W9-CIL-443

Editor:
Aileen Cantwell

Project Editor:
Dona Herweck Rice

Editor-in-Chief:
Sharon Coan, M.S. Ed.

Illustrator:
Kathy Bruce

Cover Artist:
Blanca Apodaca LaBounty

Art Director:
Elayne Roberts

Imaging:
Alfred Lau

Project Manager:
Phil Garcia

Publishers:
Rachelle Cracchiolo, M.S. Ed.
Mary Dupuy Smith, M.S. Ed.

Activities for Any Literature Unit
Primary

Authors:

Patsy Carey, Cynthia Holzschuher,
and Susan Kilpatrick

Teacher Created Materials, Inc.
P.O. Box 1040
Huntington Beach, CA   92647
©1995 Teacher Created Materials, Inc.
Made in U.S.A.

ISBN-1-55734-147-8

Table of Contents

Introduction

Activities for Any Literature Unit is a book of generic worksheets, games, art activities, and teaching ideas which will help you reinforce your students' understanding of the literature they read.

Designed for use with **children in the primary grades**, the lessons and projects may be used with a book you are reading with the class or adapted to stories in your reading series. They are ideal for core literature and for partner and individualized reading. Even though the children are reading different books, the same lesson can be applicable to all on a given day.

Ideas are developed to guide students in individualized as well as cooperative learning activities. There are three sections:

- **Before You Read**

- **As You Read**

- **After You Have Read**

In each section you will find generic worksheets to provide simple and immediate instruction as well as creative ideas to address specific learning styles. The lessons are designed to teach and reinforce such skills as basic vocabulary, sequencing, and character and plot development.

A **Teacher Resource** section provides the opportunity for you to create additional activities. Even though it is the final section of the book, it's a good idea to stop there first!

There you will find open-ended worksheets that you can quickly write on before duplicating to adapt to a specific lesson. There are additional ideas for extending the literature experience through dramatization, book writing, and art activities.

It is the hope of the authors that *Activities for Any Literature Unit* will become an invaluable tool in simplifying your entire language curriculum.

Name _____ Date _____

MY FAVORITE STORIES

What are three of your favorite stories? Write their titles on the books.

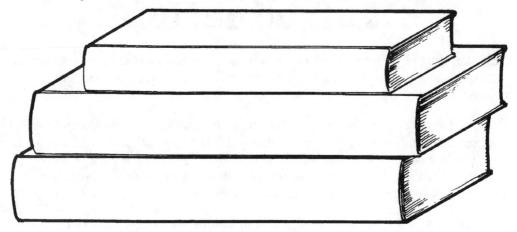

Draw a picture of something that happened in one of these books. Ask a friend to guess which book the picture tells about.

Name _____   Date_____

Book Title _____

DESIGN A BOOK JACKET

Listen as your teacher tells you the title of the book you are going to read.

Design a jacket for the book.

Directions:

1. Print the title on the lines.

2. Draw a picture about what you think will be inside.

3. Color it in bright colors.

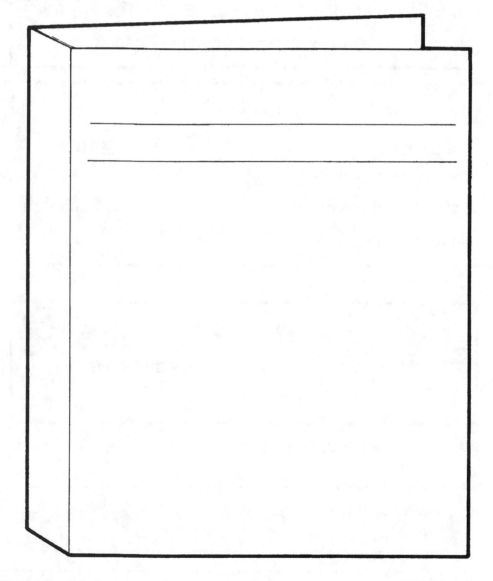

Name _____ Date_____

GETTING ACQUAINTED WITH YOUR BOOK

What is the TITLE of your book?_____

Who is the AUTHOR? _____

Skim through your book to find out more about it.

Circle the words that tell about your story.

CHARACTERS
- children
- adults
- animals
- imaginary people

SETTING

WHERE
- at home
- at school
- in the city
- in the country
- in an imaginary place

WHEN
- now
- long ago
- in the future

PICTURES
- color
- black and white

Do you think this story is about something that might happen?   yes   no

Why?_____

Do you think you will like this book?   yes   no

Why _____

Name _____ Date _____

Book Title _____

CHECK OUT THE CONTENTS

Find the **Table of Contents** in the front of your book. It tells you the page on which each chapter begins.

Directions:

1. Find each of these chapters in your Table of Contents.

2. If it has a title, write it on the line.

3. Write the page on which it begins.

Chapter	Title	Page
1.		
2.		
3.		
4.		
5.		

A Contents Puzzle: Look at the **page numbers** on the books below. If your book was open to these pages, **what chapter** would you be reading? Write its number on the open books below.

Use the back of this paper to make up your own contents puzzle to try on your friends.

Name _____ Date_____

Book Title _____

LET'S MEET THE AUTHOR

The **author** is the **person who has written your book.** It is good to know the author's name. If you like a book, you can look for another by the same author.

Directions:

1. Find four books in your library.
2. Write the title of each book and the name of the author.
3. Color the books.

Title

Author

Title

Author

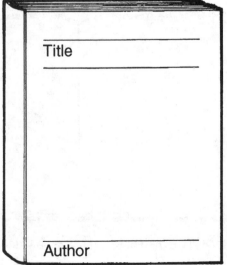

Title

Author

Title

Author

MAKING A WRISTBAND

A wristband is one good way to let your friends and family know you are reading.

Directions:

1. Print your name on the band below.

2. Look through your book. Draw a picture of something you like in the book in the circle.

3. Color your wristband in bright colors.

4. Cut out your wristband.

5. Ask someone to tape it around your wrist.

Show your friends and see if they can guess what book you are reading.

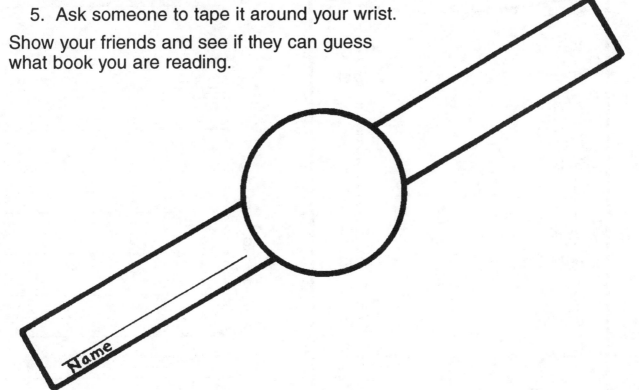

To the teacher: *You may wish to use this pattern for a "watch" to monitor each child's reading. Duplicate one copy of this page and write "HAS READ" on the top and "BOOKS" on the bottom of the circle. Then make a copy for each child. The child can write his name on the band, and color his watch. It can be laminated before it is cut out. As each child completes a book, place a small circular sticker on the face of the watch. On the sticker write how many books have been completed. The watches may be displayed in a class reading center or used on the cover of individual book report folders.*

Name _____ Date_____

ALPHABET SOUP

This is a can of alphabet soup! Circle all of these words that you can find in your story.   When you have found 15 or when your teacher stops you, write the words you have circled in ABC order.

top	every
use	forest
dog	paper
sad	quick
ask	girl
once	real
baby	mother
nice	high
where	lost
crawl	into
very	kitchen
	your

1._____

2._____

3._____

4._____

5._____

6._____

7._____

8._____

9._____

10._____

11._____

12._____

13._____

14._____

15._____

To the teacher: *To use this sheet for additional activities (e.g. 2nd letter alphabetizing or for vocabulary words related to a particular story), cut a piece of paper the size of the can and write your words on it. Tape it over the words in the can before duplicating.*

Name _____ Date _____

Book Title _____

FILLING YOUR WORD BANK

Before you begin reading, skim through your book to find the kinds of words described below. Each time you find a word described below, color a coin!

Look for a word that names a:

1. number

   _____

2. color

   _____

3. place

   _____

4. girl's name

   _____

5. boy's name

   _____

6. animal

   _____

7. sport or game

   _____

8. flower or tree

   _____

9. thing to eat

   _____

10. thing to wear

    _____

Try for some bonus bucks! Look for a word naming something made of:

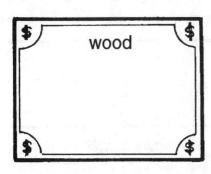

wood

glass

cloth

Name _____ Date_____

WHAT'S THE PROBLEM?

In every story the main character has a **problem to solve.** Below are some problems from stories you probably know. Draw a picture about the problem or tell how the character solved the problem. If you do not remember, use your own idea.

Problem	**How Solved**
1. Cinderella wants to go to the ball.	
2. Dorothy is lost in Oz.	
3. Beauty wants to help her father.	
4. The wicked queen wants to harm Snow White.	
5. The little mermaid wants to marry the prince.	
6. Peter Pan never wants to grow up.	

To the teacher: *You may wish to have children identify the story problems before distributing this sheet.*

Name _____ Date_____

MATCH THE SETTINGS

The setting of a story is **where** you find the characters.   Here are some characters from stories you have probably heard or read.

Draw a line to match the characters with the settings in which you would find them.

1. Little Red Ridinghood

2. Charlotte

3. Aladdin

4. The Little Mermaid

5. Beauty

6. Rapunsel

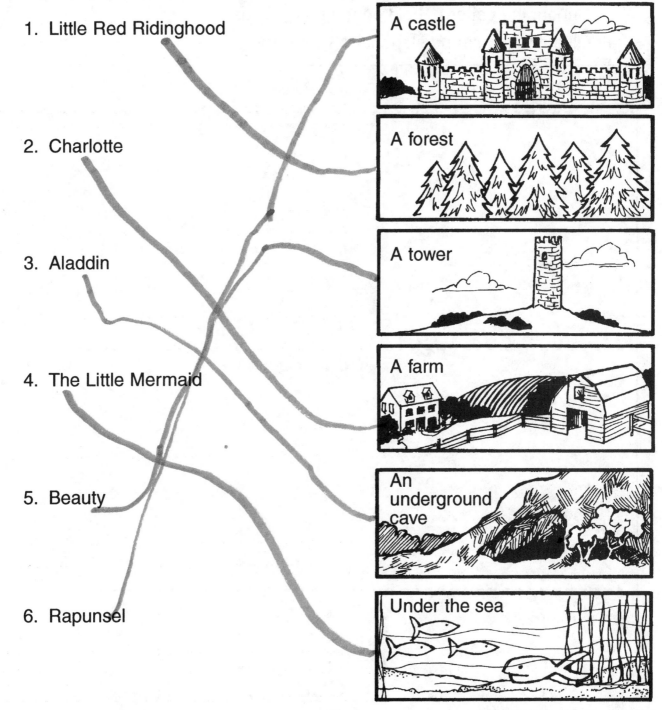

A castle

A forest

A tower

A farm

An underground cave

Under the sea

WHO??? WHERE???

Look through the first few pages of your story or listen to someone tell about it. Make a "tent" about your book to set on your desk.

Directions:

1. Draw a picture of one or more characters from your book.
2. Draw a picture of where the story takes place.
3. Cut out the pattern. Fold on the dotted lines.
4. Glue it together and stand it on your desk.

GLUE

- -

СНУВУСТЕВЗ

- -

SETTING

- -

GLUE

DESIGN A BOOKMARK

Look at the cover of your book. Skim through and look at the pictures. See if you can design a bookmark especially for this book.

Directions:

1. Draw your ideas on the pattern below.
2. Color your drawings in bright colors.
3. Carefully cut along the solid lines.
4. Fold on the dotted line.
5. Glue the sides together.

Enjoy your reading!

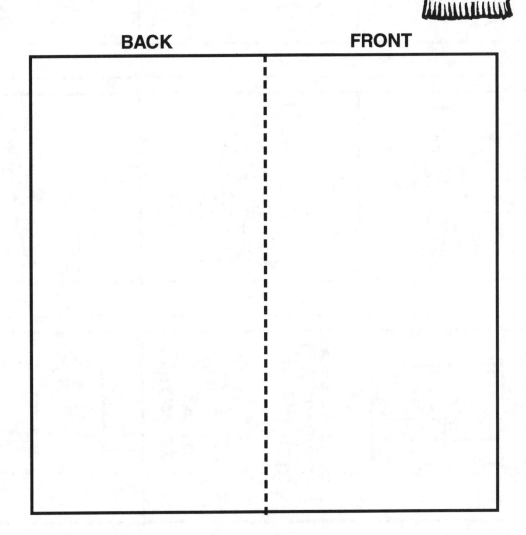

BACK   FRONT

To the teacher: *In place of #4 and #5 above, the two sides may be cut apart, mounted on construction paper, and the edges fringed. (See sample above.)*

Name _____ Date _____

WHAT CAME FIRST?

Look at each row of pictures below. They tell a story, but it is not in order.

Write **FIRST, NEXT, LAST** (or 1, 2, 3) as your teacher directs you.

_____ _____ _____

_____ _____ _____

_____ _____ _____

Name _____ Date _____

IT'S YOUR TURN TO SEQUENCE

My friend's name _____

To the teacher: Use this worksheet to reinforce sequencing. Some suggestions are:

1. Have each child draw three pictures out of sequence in each row of boxes and pass the paper to a classmate who is to write FIRST, NEXT, LAST. The second child writes his or her name on the line at the bottom of the page.

2. Have the child draw a picture in only the **one** box you direct before passing the paper.

Name LOⱰAN   Date_____

IS IT REAL OR MAKE-BELIEVE?

Look at the pictures. Write **R** in the corner box if it is **REAL**. Write **MB** in the corner box if it is **MAKE-BELIEVE.**

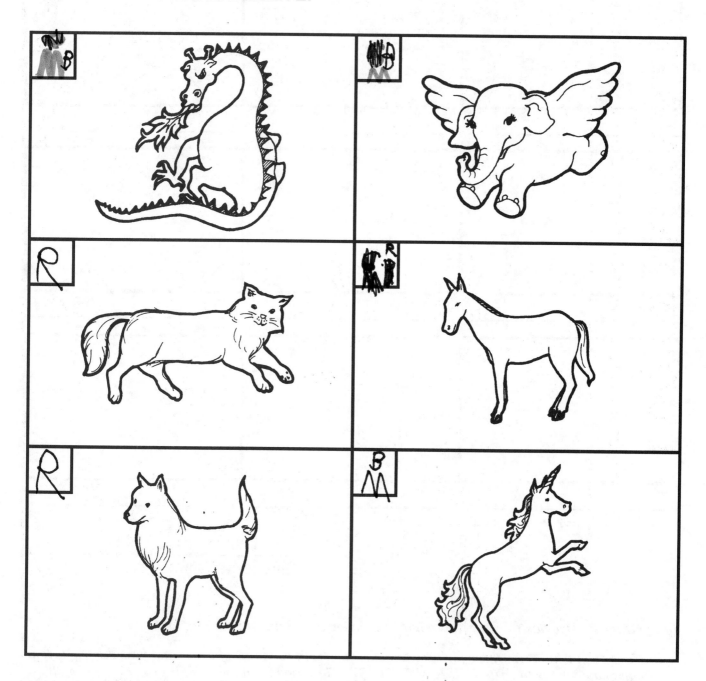

To the teacher: *You may wish to check the Teacher Resource section for hands-on ideas to teach or review this concept.*

Name _____ Date _____

I DON'T BELIEVE IT

Look at the picture. Color the things that are make-believe.

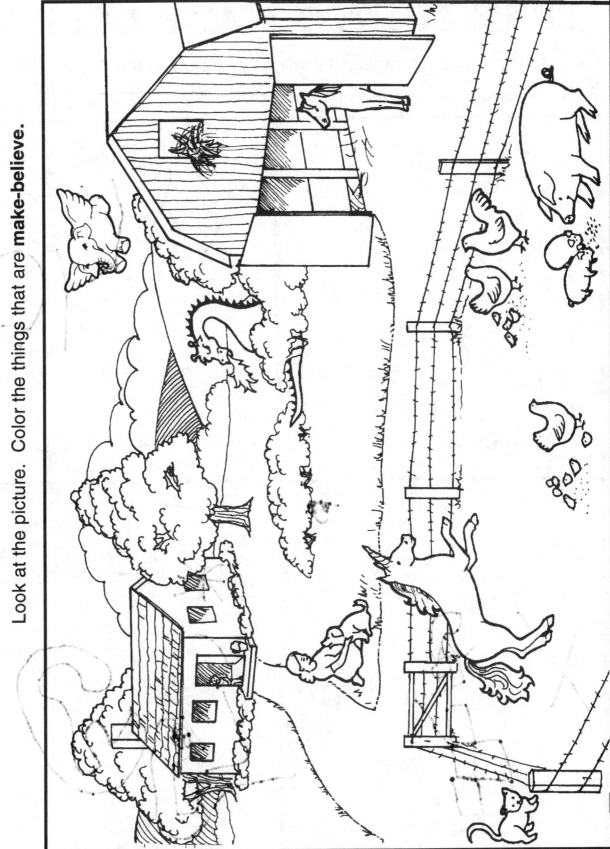

Name _____ Date_____

TURN IT INTO MAKE-BELIEVE

Look at the pictures. Draw something in each picture to turn it into **MAKE-BELIEVE.**

Name _____ Date _____

Book Title _____

YOUR NON-FICTION BOOK

The book you have chosen is **non-fiction.** That means it is about real things in the world around us.

What is your book about? _____

Why did you choose this book? _____

_____

Have you read other books about this subject? _____

List 5 facts that you know about the subject.

1. _____
2. _____
3. _____
4. _____
5. _____

List 5 facts that you hope to learn from reading this book.

1. _____
2. _____
3. _____
4. _____
5. _____

STORY-TIME GARLAND BULLETIN BOARD

This idea may be used for a reading area bulletin board and takes a minimum of teacher and student preparation.

Directions for caption:

1. Copy nine of the oval patterns on this page.
2. Copy the caption (one letter in each oval).
3. Cut eight ³⁄₄" by 5" (2 cm x 12.5 cm) strips of construction paper.
4. Cut slits in the sides of the ovals.
5. Loop the strips through, gluing to form a chain.
6. Mount it as your bulletin board caption.

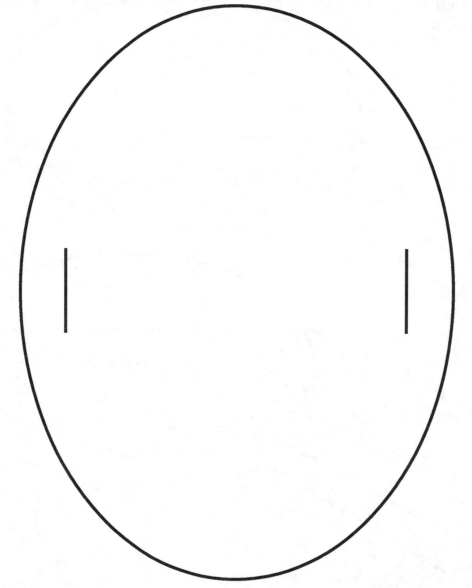

STORY-TIME GARLAND BULLETIN BOARD *(cont.)*

Setting up the board:

Give each child a folded piece of white construction paper (8"x 11" or 20 cm x 27.5 cm). On the front they are to design a book jacket for the book they are reading. Arrange the book jackets on the bulletin board.

Books in Review:

Duplicate this review form and place the copies near the board. As the children finish reading their books, they may complete this form and place it inside their book jacket for their classmates to read.

Note: Some children may need a clarification of a book review and an explanation of how to rate it positively.

MY BOOK REVIEW

Did you like this book?_____

Who was your favorite character? _____

What part did you like most?_____

_____

_____

_____

_____

_____

_____

Do you think your friends would like to read this book? _____

How many "smiles" would you give the book? Color them in. _____

_____
My name

MAKING A PENCIL TOPPER

A pencil topper will remind you of your story all day long! Color the first topper below. Now think about making a topper for a special story you are reading.

Directions:

1. Choose your favorite story character and draw it in the topper below.
2. Color it in bright colors.
3. Cut out the two toppers (not the pencils).
4. Ask your teacher to help you cut on the dotted lines and fit them over your pencils.

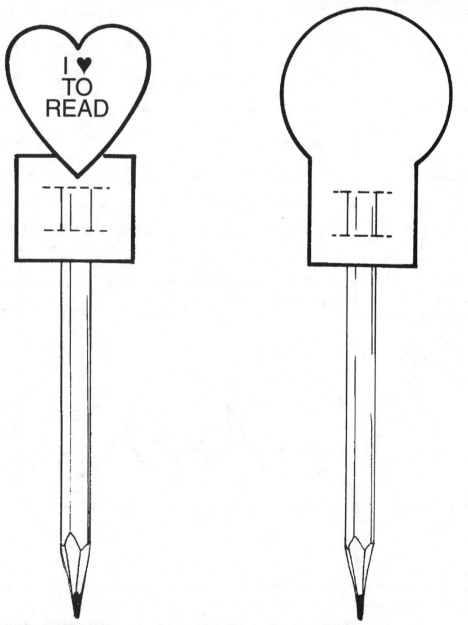

Name _____ Date_____

Book Title _____

ABC MINI-BOOK

Directions:

1. Copy the words your teacher tells you. Write one word on the line of each page below.
2. Draw and color a picture for each word.
3. Cut out the pages.
4. Staple them into a booklet in ABC order.

_____	_____
_____	_____
_____	_____
_____	_____

To the teacher: *Choose eight words to be copied from the story or suggest the children choose their own.*

Name _____ Date _____

Book Title _____

I KNOW WHAT THAT MEANS!

Directions:

1. Find a word from your story that is new to you. Write it in the first book.
2. Read the sentence where you found the word. Try to guess what the word means.
3. Write your guess on the line.
4. Now look up the word in the dictionary. If your guess was right, check the box. If not, write what the word means on the line.
5. Find 3 more new words in your story and do the same with each word.

1. _____ My guess _____ _____ _____ I guessed right! ☐ Now I know it means _____ _____ _____ _____	2. _____ My guess _____ _____ _____ I guessed right! ☐ Now I know it means _____ _____ _____ _____
3. _____ My guess _____ _____ _____ I guessed right! ☐ Now I know it means _____ _____ _____ _____	4. _____ My guess _____ _____ _____ I guessed right! ☐ Now I know it means _____ _____ _____ _____

To the teacher: *You may wish to duplicate one copy of this sheet and print in your choice of vocabulary words before duplicating the page for your children. To assign eight words, run this sheet off again on the reverse side of the paper.*

Name _____ Date_____

Book Title _____

WORD-FIND PUZZLE

It is fun to make a word-find puzzle.

Directions:

1. Choose at least eight interesting words from your story. Write them on the back of this paper.

2. Then write the same words in the puzzle grid. You may write them up, down, across, or backwards.

3. Fill in the empty squares with other letters.

4. Give your puzzle to a classmate to solve.

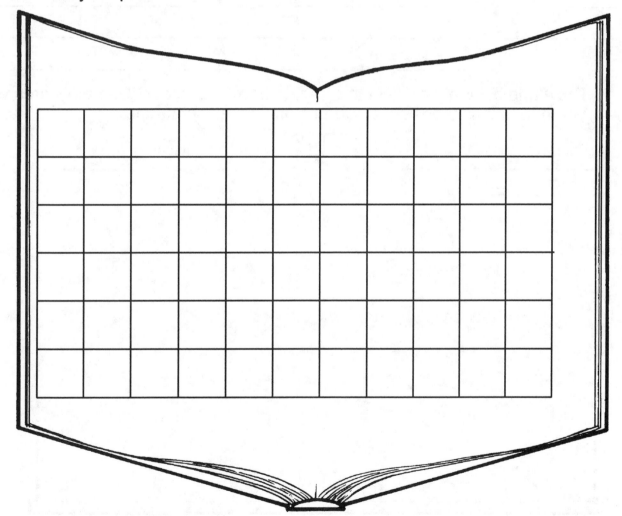

To the teacher: *You will find variations on word-find puzzles as well as a grid in the Teacher Resource section.*

Name _____ Date _____

Book Title _____

SET IT HERE

Read the beginning of your story. **Where** does it take place? This is called the **setting.**

Directions:

1. What words or phrases tell you about the **setting where your story begins?** Write them on the lines.

_____

_____

_____

_____

_____

2. Draw and color a picture of this setting from your story. Use the words you wrote to help you design it. Do **not** draw in any character.

Name _____ Date_____

Book Title _____

CHARACTER CLUES

By now you should be getting to know the characters in your story. Pick one of your favorites and find words in the story that tell something about this character. Write them on the lines.

Complete the following:

I have read to page _____. So far, my character has _____

_____

_____

I think my character will _____

_____

I think this will happen because _____

_____

Name _____ Date _____

Book Title _____

WHAT'S THE PROBLEM?

1. By the end of the first chapter you should know something about the main character. What is that character's name? _____

2. You should also know about some problem or challenge that he or she must meet. This will make up the **plot** of your story.

   Talk with your teacher or classmates about the problem in your story. Write a sentence to explain the problem.

   _____

   _____

3. Do you think the character will solve the problem?

   _____

   _____

4. How do you think the character will solve the problem?

   _____

   _____

5. What might happen to make it hard to solve this problem?

   _____

   _____

6. What might happen if he or she could not solve the problem?

   _____

   _____

7. If you were the main character, what would you do to solve the problem?

   _____

   _____

   _____

   _____

***To the teacher**: This worksheet will be a challenge to some of your children. Even those capable of meeting the challenge will benefit from a discussion of stories with which the class is familiar (e.g., fairy tales). Talk about the problem in each, obstacles that arose to complicate the action, and how the character met the challenge.*

Name _____ Date_____

Book Title _____

OFF TO A FLYING START!

Now that you have started your book, what has happened so far? Tell about it in the balloons below.

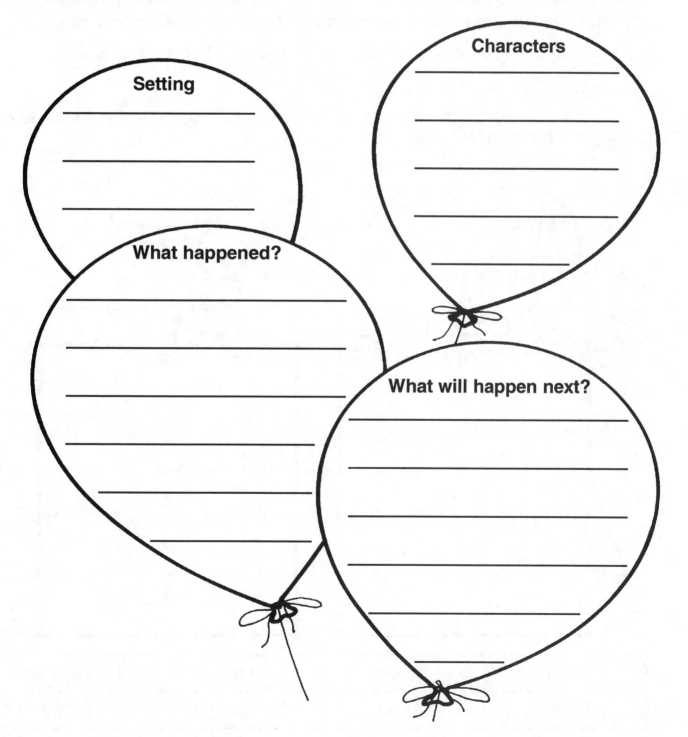

Characters

Setting

What happened?

What will happen next?

Name _____ Date_____

INTRODUCING CHARACTER TRAITS

Suppose you always smile and say hello to your friends when you see them. Don't you think they will like you? Yes, they will say that you are a friendly person. Being friendly is one **trait of your character.**   It is a **good trait.**

Suppose someone is not friendly and never smiles. That is a **bad trait.**

Directions:

1. Look at the character traits at the bottom of the page. Decide if each is a good trait or a bad trait.
2. Cut it out and paste it where you think it belongs.

GOOD   BAD

kind	selfish	not polite	likes to share
helpful	mean	never shares	happy

32

Name _____ Date _____

Book Title _____

IT'S IN THE BAG!

Think about the main character in your story. What words would you use to tell about him or her?

Directions:

1. Look in the bag of **character traits.** Choose the ones that tell about your character.

2. Print them in the boxes. (You may not fill all the spaces.)

3. Color the good traits in your favorite color.

4. Color the bad traits in another color.

kind	selfish
not polite	helpful
likes to share	mean
never shares	happy
wicked	foolish
smart	polite

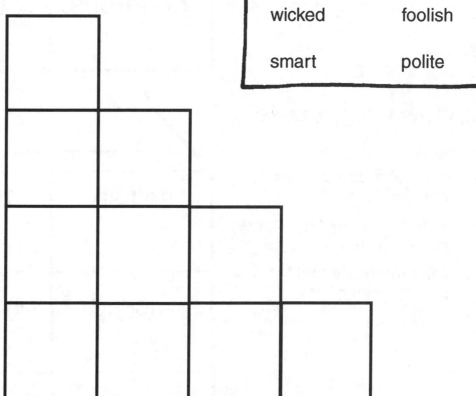

Did the character have more good traits or bad traits? _____

Name _____ Date _____

Book Title _____

MORE ON CHARACTER TRAITS

GOOD CHARACTER TRAITS

Directions:

1. Think of a **good character** from your story.
2. Write the character's name on the box top.
3. Color the **traits** that tell about him or her.

_____	
kind	helpful
happy	clever
generous	polite

BAD CHARACTER TRAITS

Directions:

1. Think of a **bad character** from your story.
2. Write the character's name on the box top.
3. Color the **traits** that describe him or her.

_____	
selfish	mean
wicked	impolite
dishonest	foolish

Name _____ Date_____

Book Title _____

PROVING CHARACTER TRAITS

Directions:

1. Write the name of the main character in the center box.

2. Think of four traits for that character. Write one in each box

3. Look through your story and find a sentence where the character shows each trait. Write it on the lines.

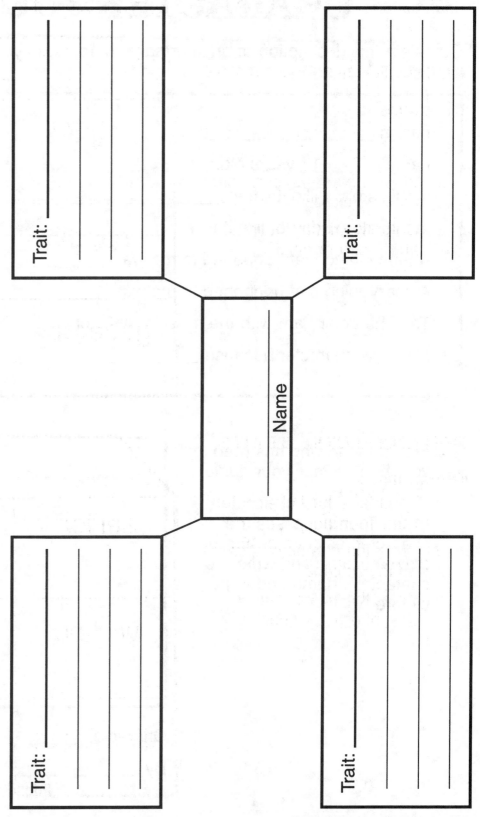

Name _____ Date_____

Book Title _____

CHARACTER RIDDLE

Complete this description of an important character in your book.

I am a _____.

I am _____ years old.

In this story, I like it when _____.

In this story I do not like it when _____.

A funny thing that happened to me was _____.

A scary thing that happened to me was _____.

The character I am with the most in this story is _____.

I like this character because _____.

Find a friend who has read your book. Pass your riddle to him or her.

If your friend guesses the character, ask him or her to draw a picture and write the character's name under the picture.

Character _____

By _____
Friend's name

Name _____ Date _____

Book Title _____

WHO DO I HEAR?

Directions:

1. Draw a picture of the main character in the circle. Write his or her name.
2. Look through your story to find five places where he or she is talking.
3. Write the words spoken in the blank bubbles.

Main character

Name _____ Date_____

Book Title _____

THE LINE IS BUSY

Directions: Choose two characters from your story and draw their pictures in the boxes. Think about a conversation they might have over the phone. Write it on the lines.

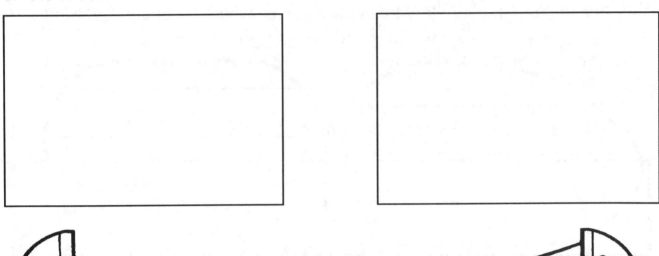

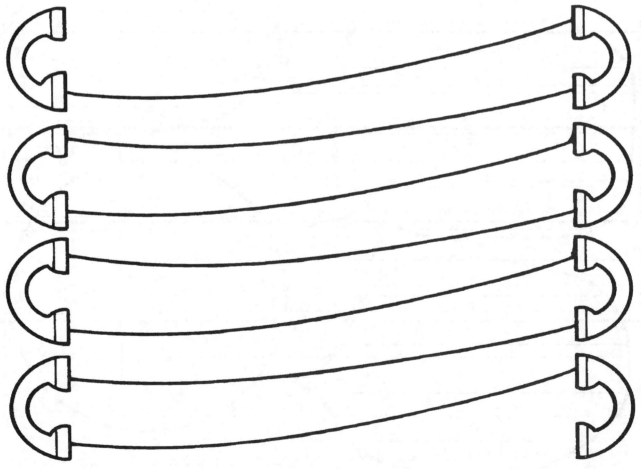

Name _____ Date_____

Book Title _____

WHO SAID THAT?

When a character talks, the words that he or she says are always written inside quotation marks (" ").

Directions:

1. Look through your story to find five places where a character is talking.

2. Write the words spoken on the lines. Be sure to begin and end the words with " ".

3. Pass your paper to a friend who has read your book. Ask that person to draw a picture of the character who is speaking.

Pictures drawn by _____

Name _____ Date_____

Book Title _____

WHO SAID IT?

You can get to know a book character by what he or she says.

Directions:

1. Pick three characters from your story. Write their names on the lines after each number.

2. Draw a picture of each one in the frames.

3. Find a sentence spoken by each character. Write their words on the lines. (Use quotation marks.)

1. _____

_____

_____

_____

_____

2. _____

_____

_____

_____

_____

3. _____

_____

_____

_____

_____

Name _____ Date_____

Book Title _____

CARTOON TIME

Think of something funny that happened in your story. Tell about it as a cartoon. Write the words your characters speak in bubbles. (They are drawn for you in the first box.)

Name _____ Date_____

Book Title _____

IT'S ABOUT TIME

Think about the main character in your story. What do you think he or she would be doing at different times of the day? Draw a picture showing your character at these hours.

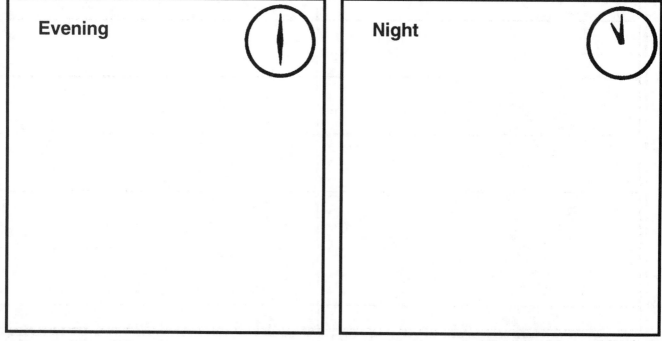

Morning

Afternoon

Evening

Night

Name _____ Date _____

Book Title _____

MY JOURNAL

Pretend you are one of the characters in the story. Choose an important day in your life and write about it.

My Journal

Date _____

◯

◯

◯

PUZZLE TIME

Directions:

1. Think of something special that happened in your story.
2. Draw it on this puzzle page.
3. Color it neatly.
4. Cut apart the pieces.

Share your puzzle with your friends.

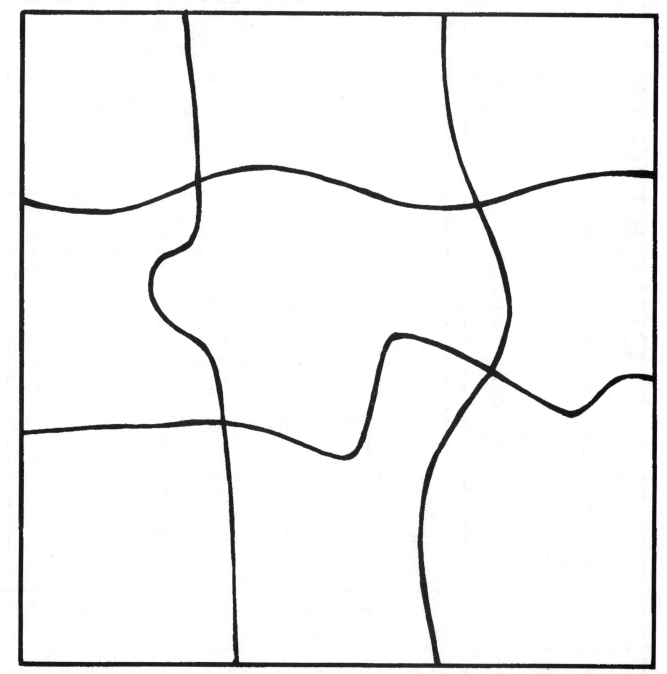

CHECKING IN

Pretend a character in your story is writing *you* a postcard.

Directions:

1. Cut out the postcard.
2. Write what the character might tell you.
3. Address it to yourself.
4. On the back, draw a picture of the place from where that character is writing to you.

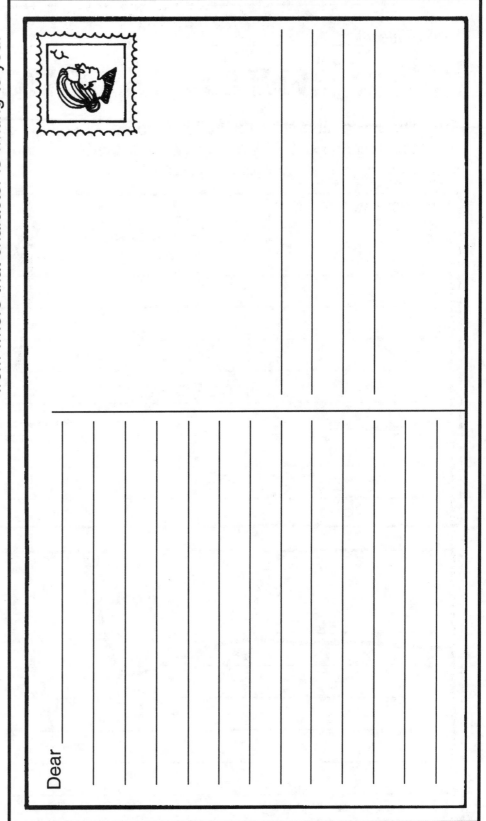

Dear _____

Name _____ Date_____

Book Title _____

WHICH IS WHICH?

Even though a story is make-believe, some things in the story could happen in real life. Think about your story. Write some things that are make-believe and some things that could really happen.

Make-Believe

_____

_____

_____

_____

_____

_____

_____

Real

_____

_____

_____

_____

_____

_____

Name _____ Date_____

Book Title _____

SPOTLIGHT ON YOU

Think of one of your favorite parts of the story. Draw a picture of **yourself** in this part of the story. Tell what **you** would do if **you** were a character in this story.

_____

_____

_____

_____

_____

Name _____ Date _____

Book Title _____

YOUR CHARACTER COMES ALIVE

Pick one of the characters from your story and answer the questions.

1. What is the name of the character? _____
2. Is it a boy or girl? _____
3. How old is he or she? _____
4. What color hair does he or she have? _____
5. What color eyes? _____
6. What else do you know about the character?

   _____

   _____

Now pretend this character turned into a **real person.** Perhaps he or she lives next-door to you! Use your imagination to answer these questions.

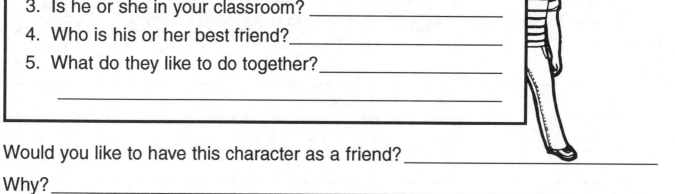

1. Where does he or she live? _____
2. Where does he or she go to school? _____
3. Is he or she in your classroom? _____
4. Who is his or her best friend?_____
5. What do they like to do together?_____

   _____

Would you like to have this character as a friend?_____

Why?_____

_____

Name _____ Date _____

Book Title _____

YOUR CHARACTER COMES ALIVE *(cont.)*

Remember, you are pretending that a character from your story has turned into a **real person.** Think what your character might like to do best. Choose his or her favorite things.

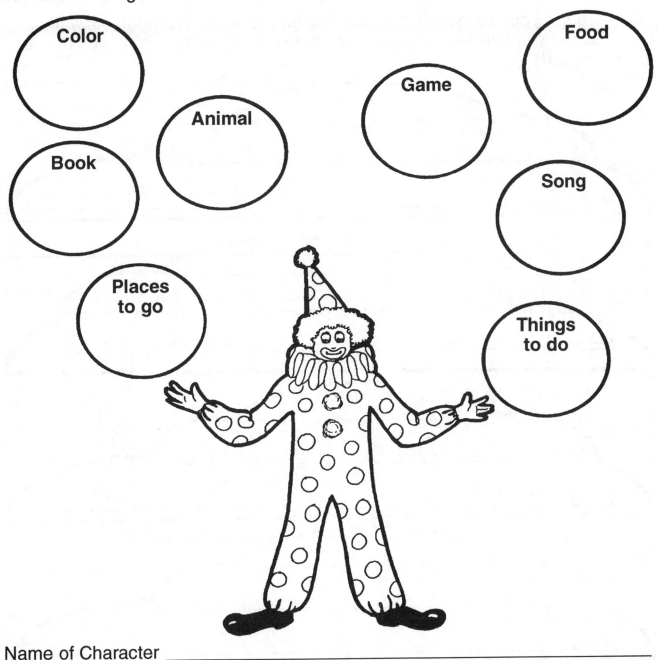

Color

Food

Game

Animal

Book

Song

Places to go

Things to do

Name of Character _____

Name _____ Date _____

Book Title _____

GETTING IN THE MOOD

Mood is part of the setting of a story. The author shows it with words. He can write about a dark night with the wind howling around an old house. That would make a scary mood for the story. He can write about a sunny afternoon in the park with children playing on the swings. That makes a happy mood for the story.

Look through **your story** to find words that let you know the mood the author wants to show. Write them in the clouds below. Then name the mood you feel from the words.

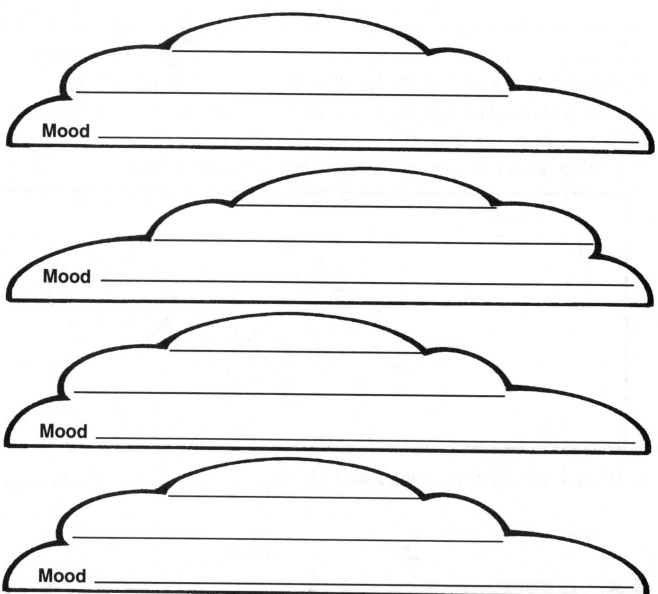

Mood _____

Mood _____

Mood _____

Mood _____

50

Name _____ Date_____

Book Title _____

THIS MUST BE THE PLACE

Think about where your story takes place. It may be in the city, at school, or on a spaceship. This is called the **setting** of the story.

Write about one **setting** from your book. **Do not name the place.**

_____

_____

_____

_____

_____

Pass your paper to a friend who has read the story. Ask that person to:

1. Read it and draw a picture of the place you wrote about.
2. Write what part of the story took place at this setting.
3. Write his or her name on the line at the bottom of the page.

1.
```
┌─────────────────────────────────────┐
│                                       │
│                                       │
│                                       │
│                                       │
│                                       │
│                                       │
│                                       │
│                                       │
│                                       │
└─────────────────────────────────────┘
```

2. This is what happened at the setting I drew. _____

_____

3. _____

Friend's name

Name _____ Date_____

Book Title _____

TAKE NOTE!

Note down the important events in this story in the order that they happened.

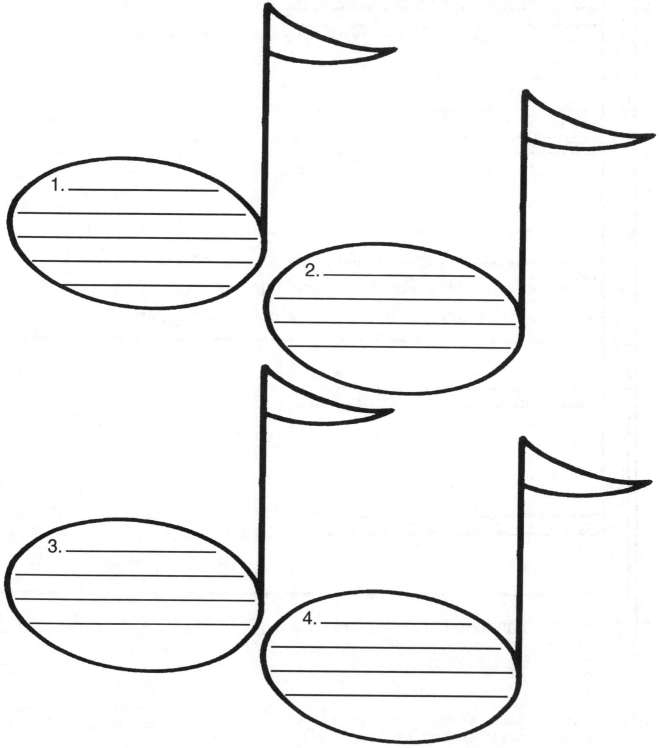

1. _____

2. _____

3. _____

4. _____

STORY LADDER

In the boxes are some things that happened in the story. Cut out the boxes.
Glue them on the ladder in the correct order to retell the story.

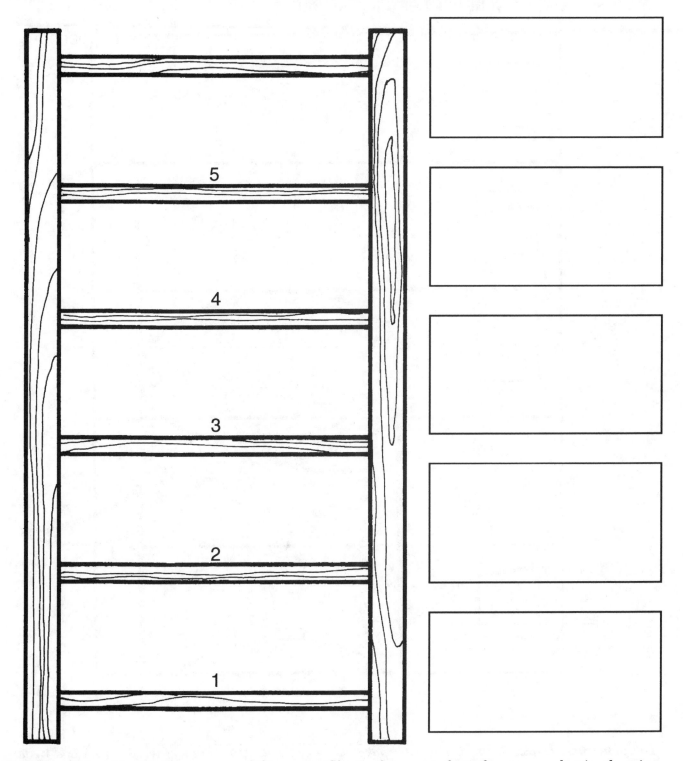

To the teacher: *Duplicate one copy of this page. Choose five events from the story, and write them in non-chronological order in the boxes before duplicating the page for the children.*

COME TO ORDER

Below are some things that happened in your story. Number them **in the order in which they happened.** Cut the strips apart. Then follow the directions on the other sheet which your teacher will give you.

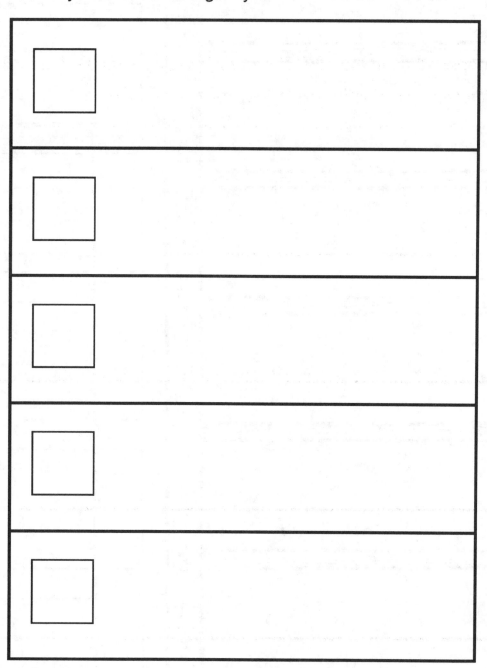

To the teacher: *Duplicate one copy of this page. Choose five or more events from the story and write them in non-chronological order in the boxes. Then duplicate copies of this and the following page for your class.*

54

Name _____ Date_____

Book Title _____

COME TO ORDER *(cont.)*

Directions:

Glue the paper strips in the correct order in the boxes on the left.

Draw a picture of each sentence in the small box on the right.

Name _____ Date_____

Book Title _____

WHAT FOLLOWS?

Read what your teacher has written on the engine. Think what came after this in the story. Write it in the next car.

To the teacher: Duplicate one copy of this page. In the engine, write an event or situation from the story before duplicating the page for your class.

As You Read: Sequence

Name _____ Date _____

Book Title _____

WHAT CAME BEFORE?

Read what your teacher has written in the rocket's exhaust. Think what happened before that in the story. Write it inside the rocket ship.

To the teacher: Duplicate one copy of this page and write an event from the story in the rocket's exhaust before duplicating the page for your children.

©1995 Teacher Created Materials, Inc.   57   #147 Activities for Any Literature Unit

Name _____ Date_____

Book Title_____

SEARCH IT OUT

What was the subject of your book?_____

What did you know about this **before** you read the book?

1. _____

2. _____

3. _____

4. _____

What did you learn from reading your book?

1. _____

2. _____

3. _____

4. _____

What other facts would you like to find out?

1. _____

2. _____

3. _____

Name _____ Date _____

Book Title _____

LET'S WRITE THE AUTHOR

Have you ever thought about writing to the author of your book? Use the space below to write down some ideas for a letter you might write.

Tell the author about yourself.

My name is _____

I am _____ years old.

I like to read books about

_____

_____

_____

_____

Tell the author about the book.

I liked the book because_____

_____

I liked it best when _____

_____

_____

My favorite character was

_____

_____

Tell about some of your wishes or feelings about the story.

_____

_____

_____

_____

_____

_____

Ask some WHY questions about the story.

_____

_____

_____

_____

_____

_____

Use your ideas to write a letter to the author of your book on the stationery paper your teacher will give you. You can make it attractive by drawing and coloring something about the book in the border. Your teacher or parent can mail it for you. Most authors will answer your letter.

To the teacher: *Duplicate the stationery on page 109 of this book. Letters may be sent to an author in care of the publisher of the book.*

TELL ME AGAIN

Directions:

1. Cut out the strips on the bold lines.
2. Glue the strips together.
3. Draw pictures and write words to retell your story.

Glue

Glue

Book title _____

Retold by _____

CHAIN OF EVENTS

Directions:

1. On each strip, write a sentence telling about one event from your story.

2. Cut the strips apart and give them to a friend.

3. Ask that person to lay them on the table in the order in which the events took place. Then have your friend glue them into a chain.

Glue	Glue	Glue	Glue	Glue	Glue

IT'S IN THE CARDS

Here is an activity you will enjoy. It will help you and a partner recall your story.

You will need:
- index cards punched on both sides
- crayons
- yarn

Directions:
1. Think about some events from the story you have read. Draw a picture of each event on a different card.
2. Print the title of your book on another card.
3. Color the pictures.

Give the cards to a friend who has read your book. Ask him or her to put the pictures in the order in which they happened. If they are in the correct order, help your friend to tie the cards together with yarn.

STEP UP TO THE PLATE!

Here is another activity you will enjoy. It will help you and a partner recall your story.

You will need:

- small paper plates punched on both sides
- crayons
- yarn

Directions:

1. Think about some events from the story you have read. Draw a picture of each event on a different plate.

2. Print the title of your book on another plate.

3. Color the pictures.

4. On the back of each plate, write a sentence telling what is happening in the picture.

Give the plates to a friend who has read your book and ask him or her to put the pictures in the order in which they happened. If they are in the correct order, help your friend to tie the plates together with yarn.

Hang them from your ceiling and think about the book you have read.

PENCIL POKE

To the teacher: *Duplicate the Pencil Poke game on this and the following page. Join the pages with tape. Color, mount on tag board, and laminate if desired. Use a punch to make holes around the perimeter. Print an event from the story beside each hole. On the back of the card, behind each event, print its chronological order in the story. Also, copy the rules, fill in the book title, and glue them on the back of the cards. (You may print on the card with a permanent fine-line marker and use nail polish remover to clean the card for other stories, or you may write on gummed labels that can be easily removed and replaced by a new set for another story.) Finally, supply a straw or pencil.*

PENCIL POKE *(cont.)*

Rules: On this card are events that you read about in this story. Your problem is to **put them in the order in which you read them.** Pick a partner to hold the card. Read the events from the story to your partner in the order you think they happened. As you read each event, poke a pencil or straw through the hole beside it. Your partner can check on the back of the card to see if you are right. Your first sentence should be "1," the next sentence should be "2," and so on.

Then, let your partner try to read the story to you.

STORY MAP

This is a story map. Can you guess the name of the fairy tale?

Try making a story map of the book you have read.

Directions:

1. Think of some important events in your story. Draw a picture of each one.
2. Tell about each picture.
3. Color the pictures.
4. Cut them out.
5. Glue them on a large sheet of paper.
6. Draw arrows to make a path from one picture to the next.

Share your map with a friend. Ask if he or she can guess the name of your story.

To the teacher: This can also be used as a cooperative learning project with a group of children working together to create a large story map. If you supply markers and a die, creative children may be encouraged to turn this project into a game.

Name _____ Date_____

Book Title _____

STORY PYRAMID

Here is a story pyramid for you to build. It will help you remember the story you have read.

Directions: Work alone or with a partner to fill in the spaces. Be sure to use only the number of words given.

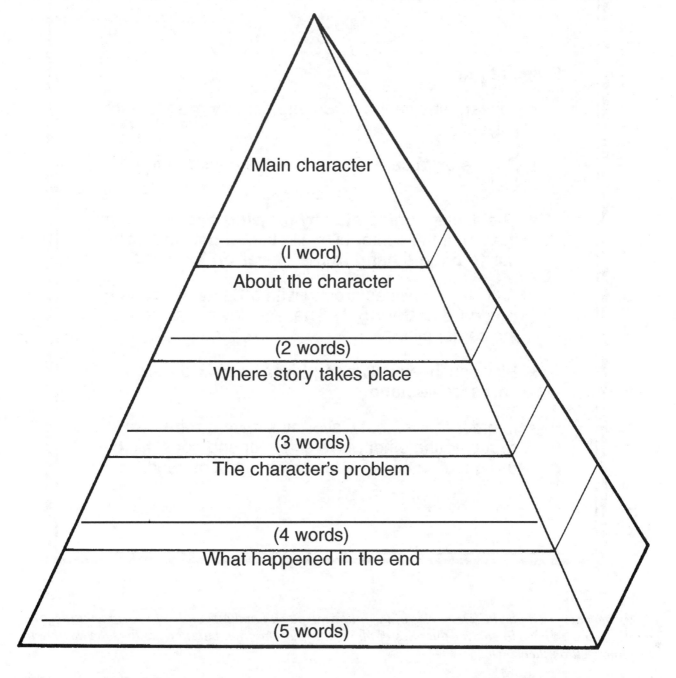

Main character

_____
(1 word)

About the character

_____
(2 words)

Where story takes place

_____
(3 words)

The character's problem

_____
(4 words)

What happened in the end

_____
(5 words)

MINI BOOK REPORT GAME

This game will give you the chance to see how much you know about the book you have just read.

This is a game for four players.

There are **six** different kinds of cards. The **object of the game is for one player to end up with one of each of the six cards.**

Rules of play:

- To start, shuffle the cards and deal **7 cards** to each player.

- Put the extra cards in a pile at the center of the table.

- The dealer **begins play by drawing one card** from the top of the center pile. He then **must trade one card from his hand to the player on his right.**

- The play continues around with **all players trading one card to the right.** The last player discards to the center pile.

- Play continues until **one player has six different cards in his hand**.

- In order to win, that player must give a **mini oral report** to the other players. He or she does this by using the six cards to tell about the book read.

To the teacher: *Duplicate **five** copies of the following page. Laminate and cut apart the cards (60 total). You may have to go over the rules of play with your children, but they should soon be able to function well on their own.*

MINI BOOK-REPORT GAME *(cont.)*

WHAT IS THE **NAME OF** YOUR BOOK?	WHERE DOES THE **STORY** TAKE PLACE?	WHO IS THE **MAIN** CHARACTER IN YOUR STORY?	WHAT **OTHER** **TWO** CHARACTERS ARE IN THE STORY?
WHAT **PROBLEM** DOES THE MAIN CHARACTER HAVE?	HOW DOES HE OR SHE **SOLVE THE** **PROBLEM?**	WHAT IS THE **NAME OF** YOUR BOOK?	WHERE DOES THE **STORY** TAKE PLACE?
WHO IS THE **MAIN** **CHARACTER** IN YOUR STORY?	WHAT **OTHER** **TWO** **CHARACTERS** ARE IN THE STORY?	WHAT **PROBLEM** **DOES** THE MAIN CHARACTER HAVE?	HOW DOES HE OR SHE **SOLVE THE** **PROBLEM?**

Name _____ Date_____

Book Title _____

PICK A PART

Tell about your favorite parts of the book.

The part that was the funniest was_____

_____

_____

_____

The part that was the saddest was_____

_____

_____

_____

The part that was the most unbelievable was _____

_____

_____

_____

The part I liked best was _____

_____

because _____

_____

_____

CREATING A STORY MOBILE

Mobiles are fun. Why not make one about the story you have read?

You will need:

- construction paper shapes (squares, rectangles, circles, triangles)
- white drawing paper
- yarn
- cardboard tube (towel or gift-wrap)
- scissors
- glue
- crayons or markers

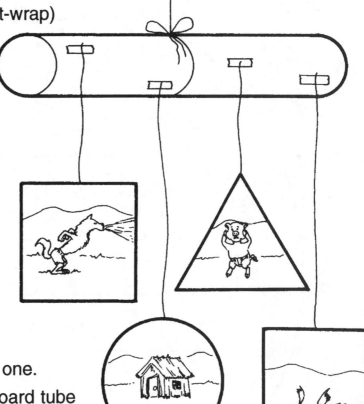

Directions:

1. Draw characters or events from your story on the white paper. Color your pictures.

2. Mount each one on a construction-paper shape.

3. Punch a hole at the top of each shape.

4. Tie a piece of yarn to each one.

5. Make four slits in the cardboard tube as illustrated.

6. Force the yarn through the slit and secure it with a knot.

7. Hang your mobile by another length of yarn tied at the center.

To the teacher: *Supply the children with patterns to cut geometric shapes from construction paper. The white drawing paper should be cut to match the size of the shapes. This project may be started in class and sent home to complete the final three directions with parent help. This is a good opportunity for the child to share his reading with his family.*

Name _____ Date_____

Book Title _____

IT MADE ME LAUGH

Look back through your book and find some things that made you laugh or smile. Write the parts you thought were funny. Then trade papers with a friend and laugh some more!

1. _____
   _____
   _____
2. _____
   _____
   _____
3. _____
   _____
   _____
4. _____
   _____
   _____
   _____

Name _____ Date_____

Book Title _____

IT'S MY FAVORITE

Write a story and decorate the border of the page to match.

My Favorite _____

_____

_____

_____

_____

_____

_____

_____

_____

_____

_____

_____

_____

_____

_____

_____

To the teacher: Duplicate one copy of this page and complete the title with an appropriate feature from the story (i.e., place, character, etc.) before duplicating the page for your children.

LIBRARY LANE

You can play this game with a friend by answering questions about your story. The one who **reaches the library first** is ready to select a new book!

Rules of play: This is a game for two players. In turn, each selects a card. If the player answers the question, he or she rolls the die to see how many spaces to move ahead. Beware of problems along the way! The winner is the first to the library door.

You forgot your card. Go back home.

You've read four books this month! Move ahead two spaces.

HOME

LIBRARY LANE *(cont.)*

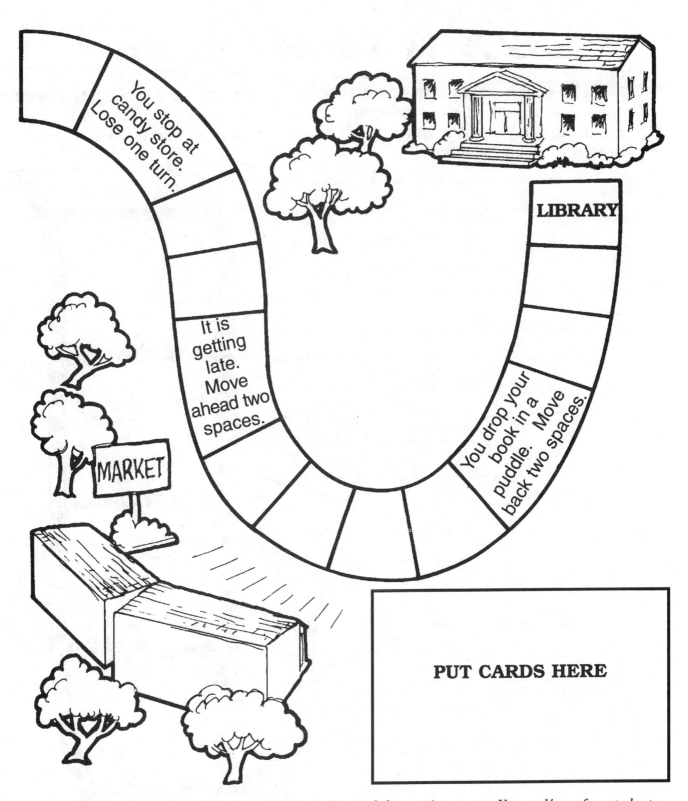

You stop at candy store. Lose one turn.

It is getting late. Move ahead two spaces.

LIBRARY

You drop your book in a puddle. Move back two spaces.

MARKET

PUT CARDS HERE

To the teacher: *To prepare the game, duplicate this and the previous page. You and/or a few students can color the two-page game board. Print questions from the book on the blank game cards. (p. 113). Mount all the game parts, laminating if possible. Supply a die and two markers.*

         #147 Activities for Any Literature Unit

Name _____ Date _____

Book Title _____

SET IT RIGHT HERE

Most stories have more than one setting. Suppose you were making a play or a movie about the book you have read. What settings would you need? Pick four. Tell about them and draw a picture of each setting. Do **not** include characters in your pictures.

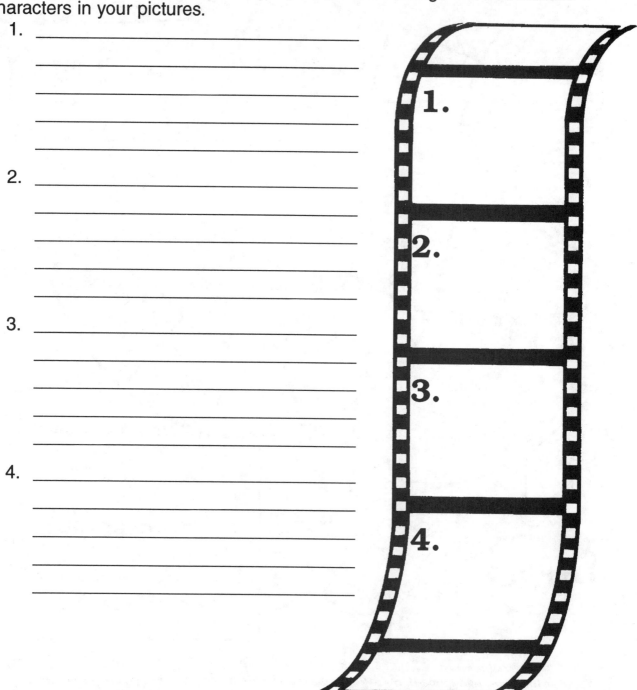

1. _____

   _____

   _____

   _____

   _____

2. _____

   _____

   _____

   _____

   _____

3. _____

   _____

   _____

   _____

   _____

4. _____

   _____

   _____

   _____

   _____

Name _____ Date_____

THE BARE BONES

_____
Title of Story

Somebody_____

Wanted _____
_____

But _____
_____

So _____
_____

At last, _____
_____

FOR BOOKWORMS

Name _____

Date _____

Title _____

Author _____

Beginning

Middle

End

Name _____

Date _____

I'VE GOT TO CROAK ABOUT IT

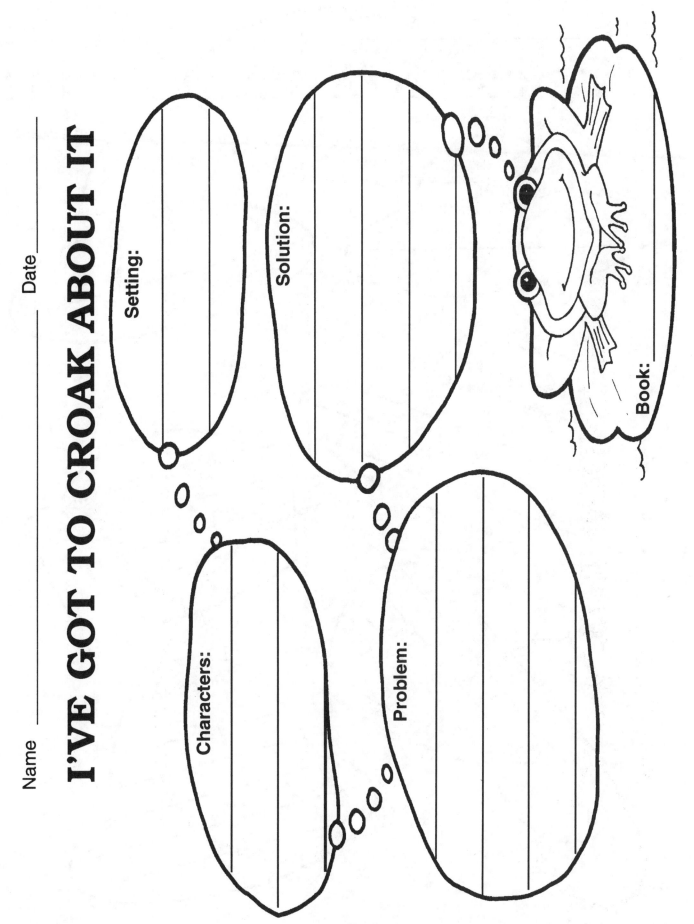

Setting:

Solution:

Characters:

Problem:

Book: _____

Name _____ Date_____

HATS OFF TO A GREAT STORY!

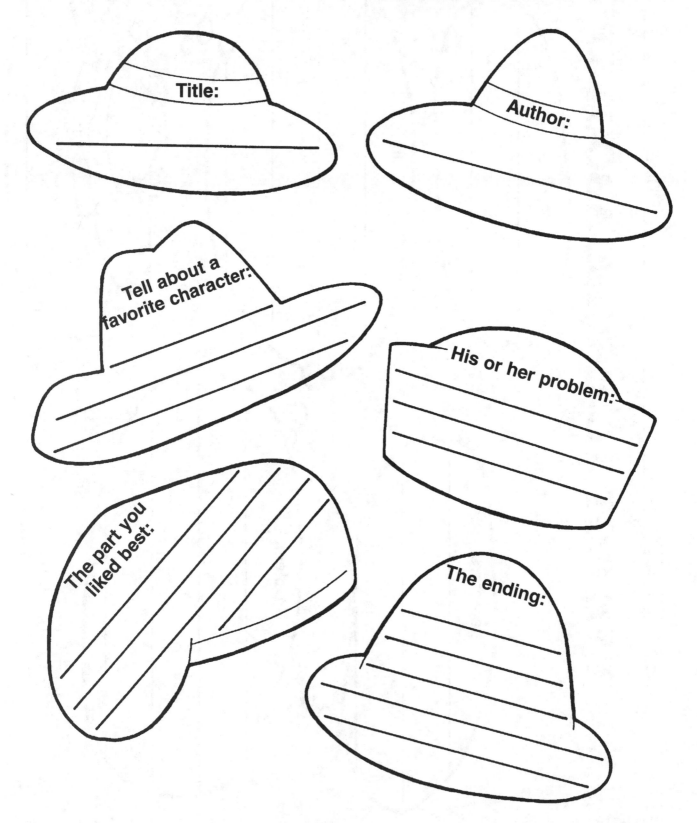

Title: _____

Author: _____

Tell about a favorite character: _____

His or her problem: _____

The part you liked best: _____

The ending: _____

Name _____ Date_____

A STORY WORTH ITS WEIGHT IN GOLD

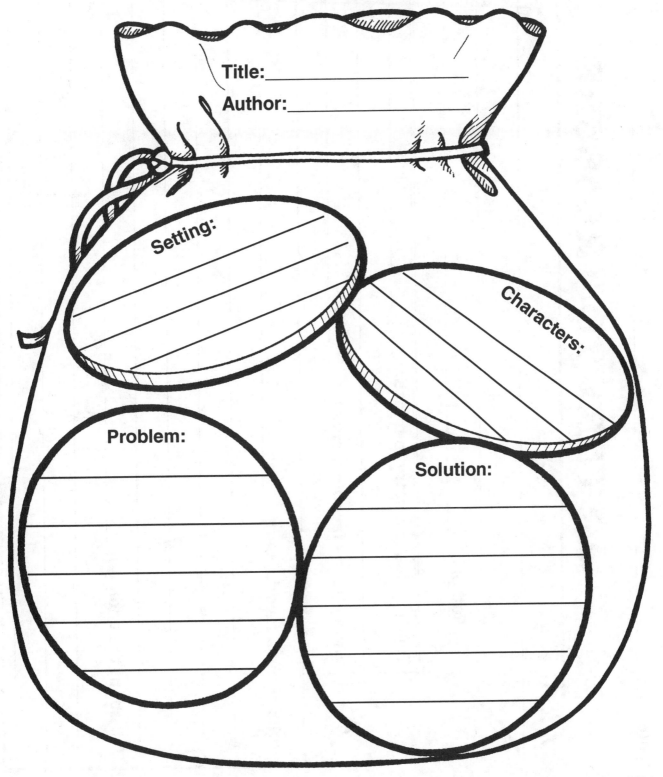

Title:_____

Author:_____

Setting:

Characters:

Problem:

Solution:

A STORY TO TREASURE

Name _____

Date _____

Title _____

Author _____

Tell why this is a story to treasure. _____

Write about a favorite character. _____

Write about a favorite part. _____

Tell about the ending. _____

82

Name _____ Date _____

A PENNY FOR YOUR THOUGHTS

Write your thoughts about the story.

Title _____

Author _____

Did it make you feel sad?

Did it have a good ending?

Would you tell your friends to read it?

Did you feel scared?

Did it make you laugh?

Names _____

TALK IT OVER

Get together with a friend who has read your book. Write a review of your book.

Book Title _____

Why we liked this book:

1. _____
2. _____
3. _____
4. _____
5. _____

What we did not like about this book:

1. _____
2. _____
3. _____
4. _____
5. _____

Do you think other boys and girls in the class would like to read this book?

_____

If you have younger brothers or sisters, do you think they would enjoy hearing

you read it aloud? _____

Name _____ Date _____

HOW DOES IT RATE?

A Review of _____

1. What I liked best about this book was _____

   because _____

   _____

2. Another thing I liked was _____

   because _____

   _____

3. What I did not like about this book was _____

   because _____

   _____

4. The best character was _____

   because _____

   _____

5. I think the book would be better if _____

   _____

   _____

6. One part I would not change is _____

   _____

   _____

7. The person I think would enjoy this book is_____

   _____

To rate the book, use a crayon to color the scale.

Super

Good

OK

Pretty good

Forget it

WHO SAID THAT?

You will enjoy playing this game with a friend who has read your book.

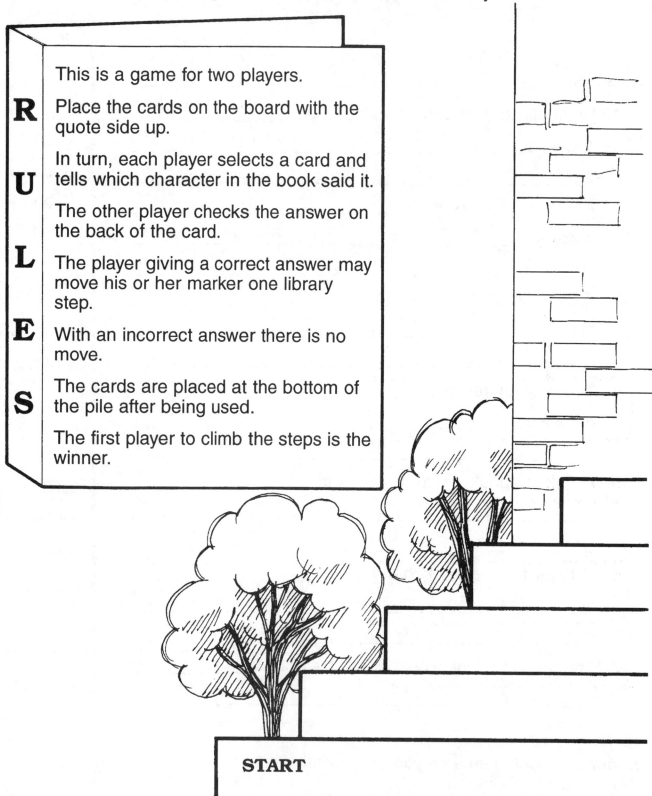

RULES

This is a game for two players.

Place the cards on the board with the quote side up.

In turn, each player selects a card and tells which character in the book said it.

The other player checks the answer on the back of the card.

The player giving a correct answer may move his or her marker one library step.

With an incorrect answer there is no move.

The cards are placed at the bottom of the pile after being used.

The first player to climb the steps is the winner.

START

WHO SAID THAT? *(cont.)*

LIBRARY

PUT CARDS HERE

To the teacher: *To prepare the game, duplicate this and the preceding page. You and/or a few children can color the two-page game board, mount it, and laminate it if possible. Print quotations from the story on the blank game cards (p. 113) with the answers on the reverse so they can be checked. Laminate the cards for long life. Supply two markers.*

Name _____ Date_____

Book Title _____

CHARACTER WEB

You can see this a special kind of web. It is a **character web.**

Directions:

Draw a picture of the main character in the center circle. In each of the spaces answer the question about the character.

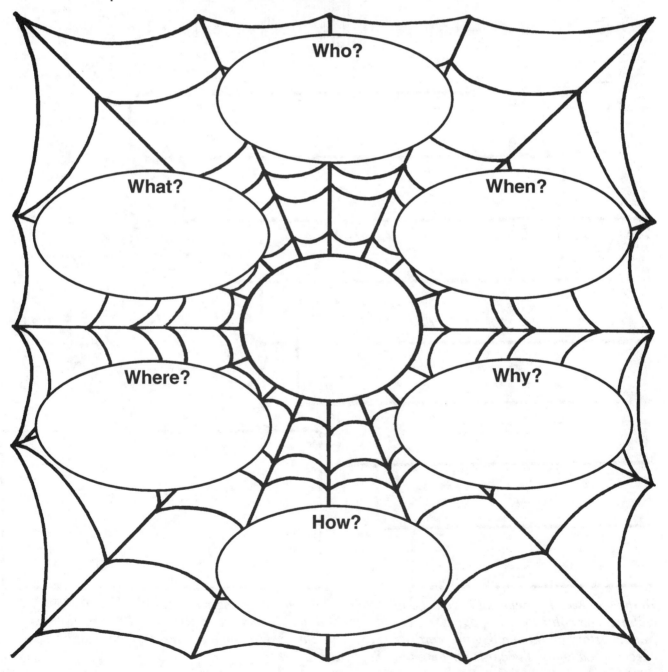

Name _____ Date_____

Book Title _____

WHAT A CHARACTER

Directions:

1. Draw your main character's picture in the circle.

2. Think about the character at the beginning of the story. Copy some sentences to show how he or she acted when the story began.

3. Think about the character at the end of the story. Copy some sentences to show how he or she acted near the end of the story.

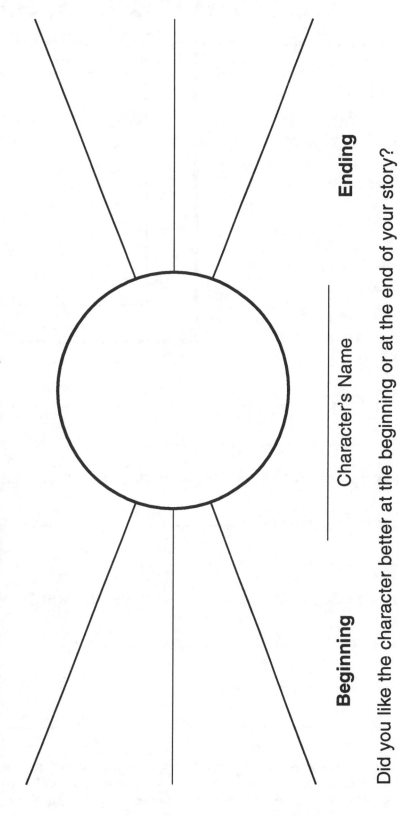

Ending

Character's Name

Beginning

Did you like the character better at the beginning or at the end of your story?

Why? _____

Name _____ Date_____

Book Title _____

BLUE RIBBON AWARD

A blue ribbon is very special. It is awarded only to the very best.

Think of a character in a story that deserves a blue ribbon. What is the name of that character?

_____

Draw his or her picture in the box.

Did this character do anything in the story to help others? _____

If so, tell about it._____

_____

Did the other characters in the story seem to really like this character? _____

How did they show this? _____

_____

Why do you think this character deserves an award? _____

_____

_____

_____

To the teacher: *This page may be used to prepare for a culmination activity. By using this page and the two following pages along with the letter writing idea on p.108, you can stage a presentation ceremony for the award. Perhaps you might even serve the character's favorite food!*

Name _____ Date_____

Book Title _____

BLUE RIBBON AWARD *(cont.)*

Think about why you would like to give a blue ribbon award to a character in your book.

Directions: Complete this form to nominate him or her for the award. Practice reading it over. Be prepared to read it to your class.

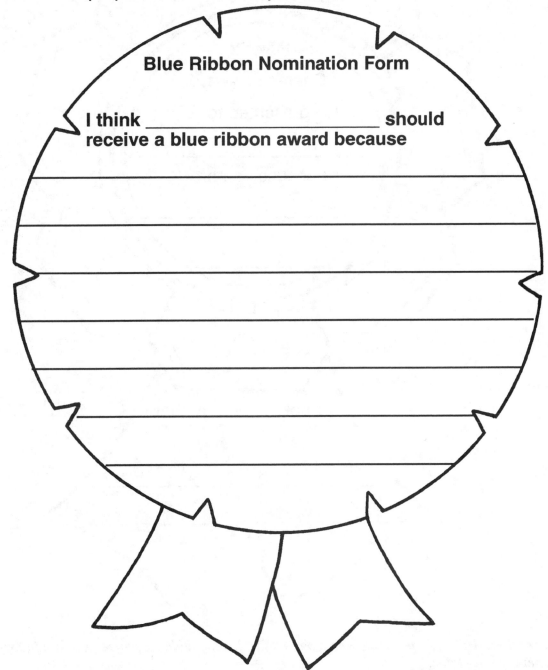

Blue Ribbon Nomination Form

I think _____ should
receive a blue ribbon award because

BLUE RIBBON AWARD *(cont.)*

Fill in the blue ribbon award on this page and color it as a special prize for your favorite character.

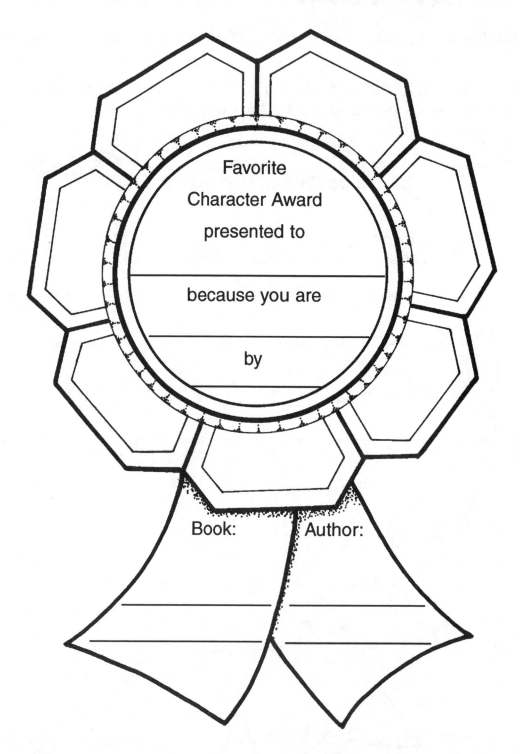

To the teacher: This may be cut out and mounted for display and/or become part of a favorite character memory book.

Name _____ Date _____

Book Title _____

COULD IT BE?

Could a story like this one really happen? _____

Tell three reasons for your answer.

    1. _____

    2. _____

    3. _____

Could a story like this really happen to **you?** _____

Why or why not? _____

_____

_____

Would you **like** to have this story happen to **you?** _____

Why or why not? _____

_____

_____

Suppose this story was going to happen to you. Tell how you would like it to end. _____

_____

_____

Name _____   Date_____

Book Title _____

PRESTO CHANGE-O!

Draw a picture of your main character in the frame.

Think about a part of the story where the main character did something you really liked.   Write about it on the lines below.

_____
_____
_____
_____
_____
_____
_____
_____
_____
_____
_____
_____
_____
_____
_____
_____
_____

Name _____ Date_____

Book Title _____

PRESTO CHANGE-O! *(cont.)*

Now it is time for the Presto Change-o!

If the main character in your story was a person, DO THIS!

Change that character into an animal! Draw a picture of the character as an animal. Write about the same part of the story using this animal as the main character.

If the main character in your story was an animal, DO THIS!

Change that character into a person! Draw a picture of the character as a person. Write about the same part of the story using this person as the main character.

My "Presto Change-o"

_____
_____
_____
_____
_____
_____
_____
_____
_____
_____

_____
_____
_____
_____
_____

Name _____ Date_____

Book Title _____

NAME CHANGE?

Do you like the title of your book?_____

Why do you think the author gave the book
this title? _____

_____

_____

_____

_____

Write three new titles for the story. Be sure they give the reader a good idea of
what the story is about.

1. _____

2. _____

3. _____

Which of your titles do you like best? _____

Why?_____

_____

_____

Do you like your title better than the title the author chose for the book? _____

Why?_____

_____

_____

_____

96

Name _____ Date_____

Book Title_____

HERE COMES THE CABOOSE!

Think of a new ending for your story.
Write it on the caboose.

Name _____ Date _____

SEQUEL IN PROGRESS

Think about the book you have just read. Fill in the chart below.

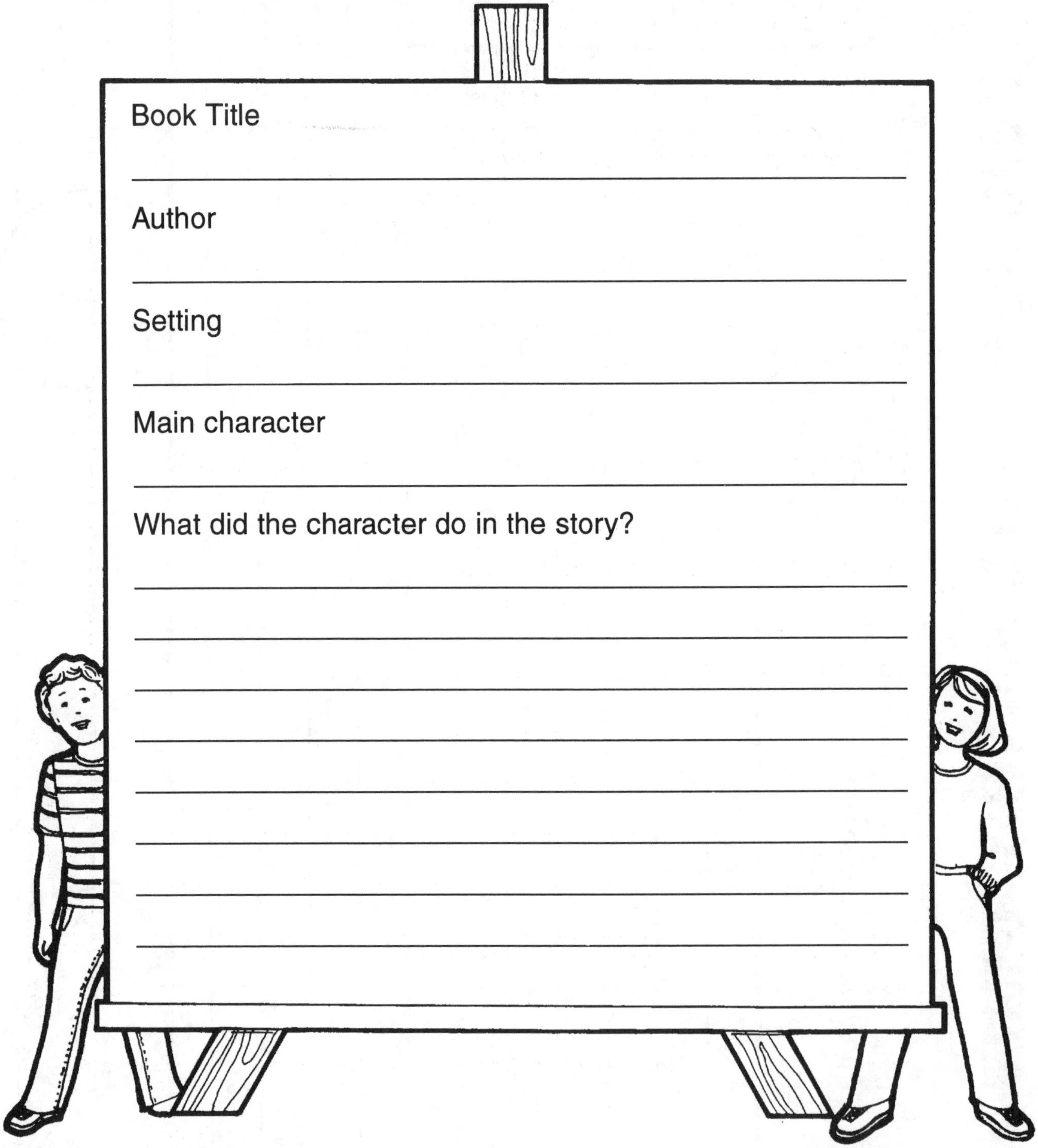

Book Title

_____

Author

_____

Setting

_____

Main character

_____

What did the character do in the story?

_____

_____

_____

_____

_____

_____

_____

To the teacher: *Duplicate this and the following page to plan a book sequel. If you have the proper equipment, you may wish to enlarge the pages to be used as a group lesson.*

Name _____ Date_____

SEQUEL IN PROGRESS *(cont.)*

You have been chosen to write a sequel to the story you have just finished reading. Think about how you will do it.

Title of the new book you will write:

_____

Your name (the author):

_____

Main character's name:

_____

How long after the first story ended will your story begin?

_____

Where will the new story take place?

_____

What will your character do next?

_____

_____

_____

_____

_____

_____

Name _____ Date_____

SEQUEL IN PROGRESS *(cont.)*

Remember, you are writing a sequel to the book you have just read. Write or draw some events that will happen in your book on the pages below.

I am planning to write a sequel to the book _____

_____

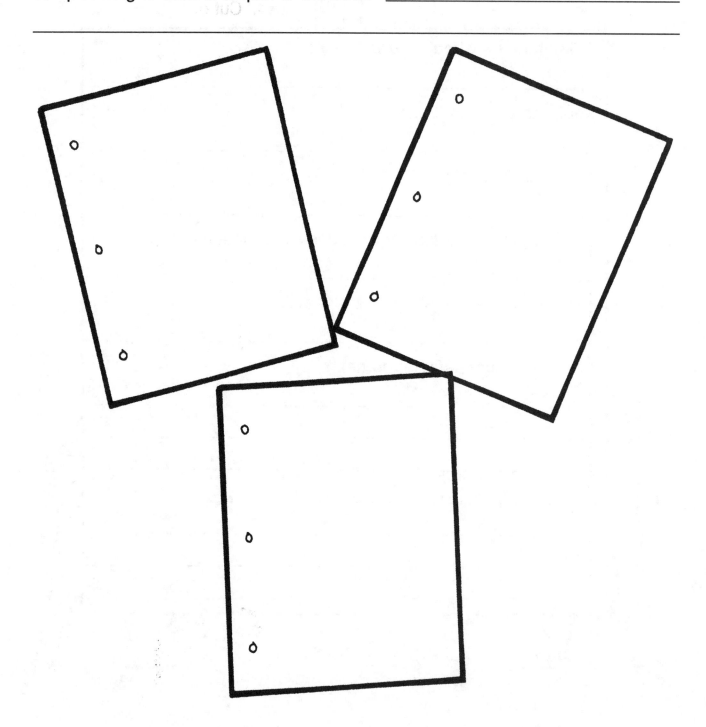

SEQUEL IN PROGRESS *(cont.)*

Now it is time to plan the cover of your book's sequel.

Directions:

1. Carefully print the title of your new book.

2. Print your full name as the author.

3. Draw and color a scene from your book.

4. Cut out the cover.

To the teacher: *You may wish to check in the Teacher Resource chapter for book-making ideas.*

THE BOOKS I HAVE READ

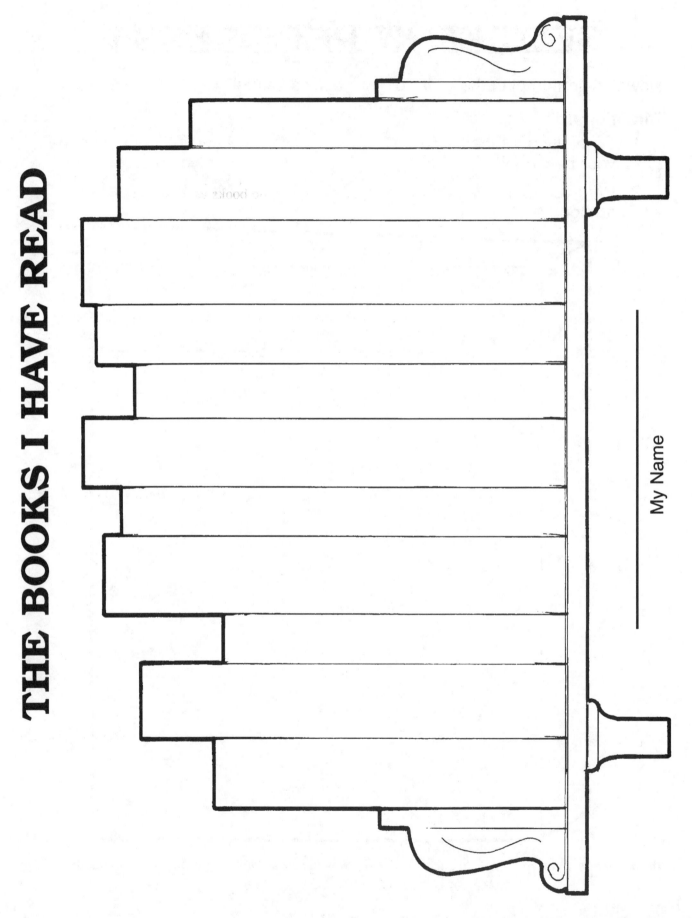

My Name _____

READING IS FOREVER

KEEPING RECORDS

Children take pride in their reading success. You can begin with simple record-keeping. At the beginning of a school year you can organize a system for keeping track of your children's reading progress. This may be done in a variety of ways.

- A **simple record** of books read can be achieved by duplicating the previous page, mounting it in or on the cover of a folder, and having each child record the books as they are read.

- Any or all of the pages for **book reports** in the "After You Have Read" section can be kept in a child's reading folder.

- Each child can create a **favorite character book**. It can be made up of the Blue Ribbon character awards (page 92).

- Class activities may include a **reading chain**, each link representing a book that has been read. Have the children write their names and the name of each book on an 8" by 1" (20 cm x 2.5 cm) strip of construction paper. Each strip is circled into a link and stapled or glued to another link. The chain grows in length on the wall or bulletin board as the weeks progress.

  You may wish to reward your class for their good efforts at a designated period of weeks.

GETTING CREATIVE

A good book can motivate children to express their creativity.

- Projects found throughout this book and elsewhere can be turned into **long-lasting mementos** of a favorite character or story. Activities that take effort on their part (and yours!) will be treasured by both children and parents.

- Groups of children can create **murals** of favorite stories with paint or by collage.

- A **Character Clue Day** can be planned on which each child brings an object related to a book character. The class tries to guess the character. For example, a shiny red shoe could lead to Dorothy from *The Wizard of Oz*.

- As the year progresses, favorite book characters can be turned into **life-sized paper-doll models.** Have the children work in partners. One child lies on a large sheet of paper while the partner traces his or her outline. When models are colored, they can be seated on chairs. As the class interviews each character, its "creator" can give the answers.

Ideas are limited only by your imagination. A good teacher can show the child that *reading is forever!*

DRAMATIZATION

Dramatizing a story is not only fun for children, but it can greatly improve their reading skills.

Stick Puppets

Materials: white tagboard, paper, craft sticks or straws, scissors, tape or glue

To prepare:

1. Ask the children to name the characters and objects that play important parts in their stories.

2. Have them draw and color the characters on white paper. They may create their own designs or use the outlines of the figures (pages 138–142). Some characters may need more than one shape.

3. Help them mount their figures on tagboard and secure them to the ends of craft sticks or straws.

To proceed:

- Children are usually very comfortable projecting their ideas through puppets.

- Initially, the puppets may be used to **teach character traits** or actions. As the teacher makes statements about the characters, children can hold up the correct puppets.

- The class can then be divided into small groups to **prepare assigned scenes** from the story. One child can be the narrator, reading from the book as the others operate their puppets.

The children's creativity will quickly take over.

- They can experiment with the puppets, **retelling the story** in their own words.

- They can be innovative by **adding new situations** to the story.

- They can use their book and practice **recognizing dialogue** as they read the character parts aloud.

- They can even use their puppets in **presenting a TV commercial** for their book.

DRAMATIZATION *(cont.)*

Stick Puppet Theater

The children will enjoy having a "home" for their puppets.
(Make one theater for every 2-4 children.)

Materials: colored poster board (¹/₂ sheet for each theater)

To prepare:

1. Cut a piece of colored poster board in half.

2. Fold the sides back.

3. Cut a "window" in the front panel.

4. Let the children personalize and decorate their own theaters.

Shadow Play

In a shadow play, the children use the silhouettes of their puppets to represent objects and characters from a story. Place a simple silhouette representing a character from the story on an overhead projector or in front of another light source. Project it onto a screen or wall. Have the children guess who it represents. They will easily be motivated to use their puppets or create others to make shadows of their own.

Before presenting their play, give the children the opportunity to practice projecting their silhouettes in front of a light source.

SUPER, FANTASTIC, NEVER-FAIL, PRACTICALLY PERFECT PLAY DOUGH

Children love to work with clay and some book characters lend themselves readily to this medium.

For example, any of the animals in *Where the Wild Things Are* by Maurice Sendak can be a perfect model. The finished product may be left free-standing or affixed to a small piece of wood for a more lasting memento of the story. In the latter case, you may wish to eliminate the food coloring from the recipe and spraypaint the background wood in a bright color.

Ingredients:

- 3 cups (750 mL) flour
- 1½ cups (375 mL) salt
- 6 tsp. (30 mL) cream of tartar
- 2 tbsp. (30 mL) oil
- 3 cups (750 mL) water
- food coloring (optional)

To prepare:

1. Mix flour, salt, and cream of tartar in a large mixing bowl. Add oil, water, and food coloring. Mix thoroughly.

2. Cook in an electric skillet on low heat. Keep cooking and knead until it is the consistency of bread dough and dry to the touch.

3. Remove from pan. Continue to knead. Store in airtight baggies or plasticware. It will remain soft and pliable for six months.

Enjoy!

STORY SCENE

A shoe box can be the center of two projects the children will enjoy.

The teacher or an older child can make samples that the primary children can copy with some assistance.

DIORAMA

Materials: a shoe box (without the lid), construction paper or shelf paper, lightweight tagboard, scissors, glue, tape, crayons or markers, magazine pictures (optional), Contac® paper to cover outside of box (optional)

Directions:

1. Cut out one side out of the shoe box.

2. Cover the outside of the box, if you wish.

3. To make a pattern for the inner walls, lay the box on the construction paper and measure the size of the three outer sides. Fold the paper around the box and cut around the outline.

4. Decorate these inner walls with drawings or magazine pictures.

5. Glue the walls in place inside the box.

6. Cover the floor of the box in the same way.

7. Tagboard and construction paper may be used to make other free-standing pictures for the scene. Consider adding other materials like foil, cotton balls, fabric, yarn, clay, and twigs (for trees).

8. Label with the title, author, and artist's name.

PARADE FLOAT

Here is where the **lid** of the shoe box comes into play. Replace the shoe **box** with its **lid**, and using the same materials as for the activity above, direct the children to make a **float** for their book. They can cover the **lid** appropriately, add free-standing forms, and even add wheels if they wish!

Either of these projects may be started in class and sent home to be completed with a parent's help. They will enjoy it while the children will have the opportunity to share their reading accomplishments.

 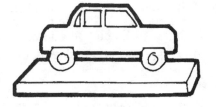 

USING STATIONERY AND CARDS

IDEAS FOR USING THE STATIONERY (page 109)

The children may use the stationery sheet on p.109 for a variety of activities. Suggest they:

- Write to the author of their book (page 59).
- Write a fan letter to their favorite character.
- Write to invite a character to a special celebration where he or she will be presented with a Favorite Character Award (page 92).
- Write a letter from one character to another in the story.
- Write a letter from a character in the story to another telling about what he or she is doing a year after the story has concluded.
- Write a letter from a character to someone asking for help he or she needs to do something in the story.
- Write a thank-you letter from a character in the story.
- Write to recommend their book to a friend.

IDEAS FOR USING THE OPEN-ENDED CARDS (pages 110–113)

These open-ended cards are ideal in teaching the differences between two concepts.

- **REAL and MAKE-BELIEVE** responses help children to distinguish the difference when these two ideas are blended into the same story.
- **YES and NO** responses provide practice with these same critical thinking skills.

  A **YES** statement reflects an idea the child knows about, appreciates, or understands, while a **NO** statement reflects an idea he dislikes, disputes, or does not comprehend. While using the flash cards, you can ask the child to supply a reason for his answer.
- **NOW and THEN** responses can be helpful when the setting of the story takes place in a past or future time.
- **LITERAL and INFERRED** responses can help introduce the meaning of simple idioms. (You may wish to call them TRUE and FALSE).
- **FACT and OPINION** responses can continue to develop critical thinking skills with more capable learners.

Here are more specific instructions for using these pages. **REAL and MAKE-BELIEVE** will be used as an example.

FLASH CARDS (page 110)

To prepare: Duplicate one copy of the page and write on the cards before duplicating a set for each child. Glue the "REAL" cards to one color of paper and the "MAKE-BELIEVE" cards to another, laminating if desired.

To proceed: Read several different statements — some **REAL,** some **MAKE-BELIEVE.** Children hold up the appropriate card after each statement is read.

CUT AND PASTE SQUARES and BOARDS (pages 111–112)

To prepare: Duplicate one copy of the squares (p. 112). and one copy of the boards (p. 111). Write phrases or draw pictures on the squares (p. 112). Six are to be real, six make-believe. Write **REAL or MAKE-BELIEVE** at the top of the boards. Duplicate one of each sheet for every child.

To proceed: The children will cut the squares apart and glue them on the proper side of the boards.

GAME CARDS (page 113)

These cards may be used for many purposes, especially for creating the games in the "After You Have Read" section.

STATIONERY

FLASH CARDS

CUT AND PASTE BOARDS

CUT AND PASTE SQUARES

GAME CARDS

VENN DIAGRAM

In a **Venn diagram** two people, places, or things are compared and contrasted. Two overlapping circles are most often used to contain the comparisons, but other shapes may be used as well. The shared portions of the circles list the qualities that are held in common, while the opposite portions list qualities that are unique to one subject.

Fairy tale characters make good sources to introduce a Venn diagram. Guide your children through some comparisons such as the one below.

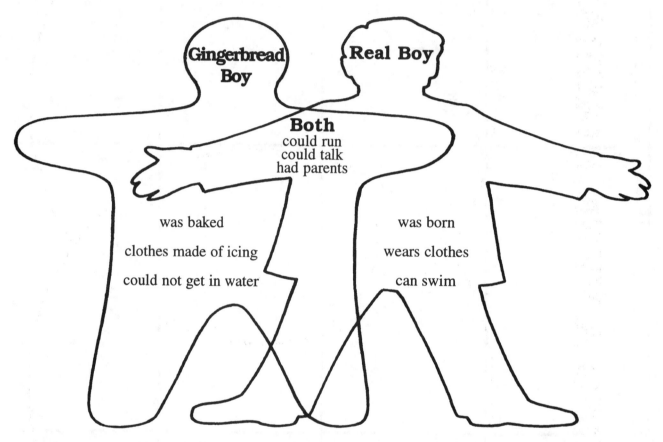

Duplicate the Venn diagram (p.115) and assign two ideas for your children to compare.

SUGGESTIONS FOR COMPARISON

- Fictional character with a real person
- Fictional character with yourself
- One fictional character with another in the story
- A fictional character with one in a different story
- Two settings from the story
- The story setting with a place you have visited
- The time period of the story with the present time period
- One story with another

Name _____

Date _____

MAKING A VENN DIAGRAM

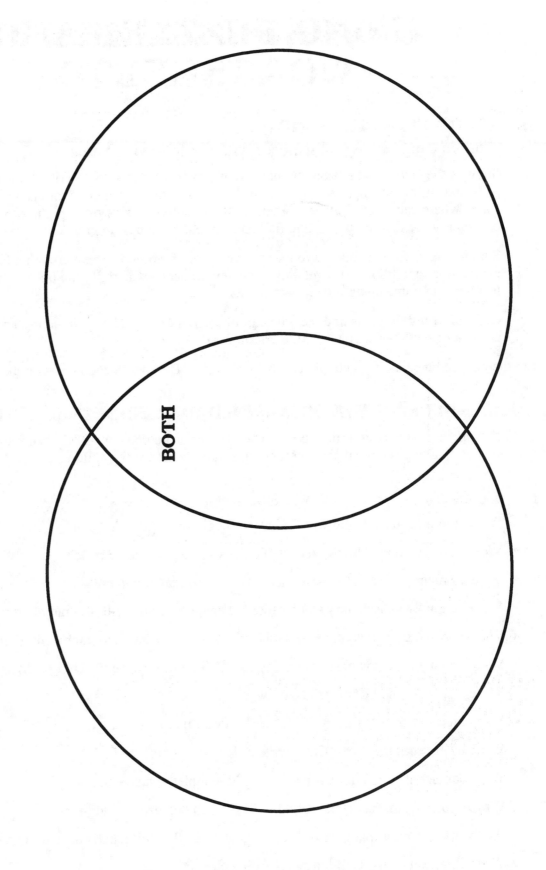

BOTH

USING PUZZLES AND WORKSHEETS

IDEAS FOR USING THE GRID (page 117)

The children can create word searches with the following variations.

- Suggest they choose at least eight interesting words from the story, write the words in the puzzle grid, and fill in the empty squares. Then he or she writes a sentence for each word, *leaving a space* where each word belongs. Each child trades his puzzle with a partner to see if the partner can supply the missing words and find them in the word puzzle grid.

- Supply words for the children to make a word search around a theme relating to a character (for example, a search for words relating to spiders to keep a Charlotte fan busy). The more capable learners can come up with their own words.

- Give the children words and see who can fit them into a word search, taking up the smallest amount of rectangular space on the grid.

Let the children try making a simple crossword puzzle. They will need help with the numbering.

IDEAS FOR USING THE OPEN-ENDED WORKSHEETS (pages 118-122)

Use the worksheets to create follow-up as needed. Duplicate one copy of the page and write your questions or challenges on that sheet before duplicating a set for the children.

For example:

- Write initial sounds. Child will find words beginning with that sound.

- Write color words on the worksheet. Child will use crayons to match.

- Write number words on the worksheet. Child will match numerals.

- Write scrambled vocabulary words from the chapter. Child will unscramble the words.

- Write vocabulary words on the worksheet. Child will print and match definitions.

- Write synonyms, antonyms, or homonyms. Child will provide matching words.

- Write a short riddle. Child prints answer.

- Write an event from the story. Child writes event that comes after.

- Write event from the story. Child writes what comes before.

- Write statement ending in *because*…. Child completes statement.

- Write quotes from characters. Child writes which characters said them.

- Write clues about a character on the worksheet. Child will match character name.

- Write character trait. Child matches with a character.

- Write a group of nouns from the story. Child will provide appropriate adjectives or verbs.

PUZZLE GRID

Name _____ Date _____

Book Title _____

I SEE THE LIGHT

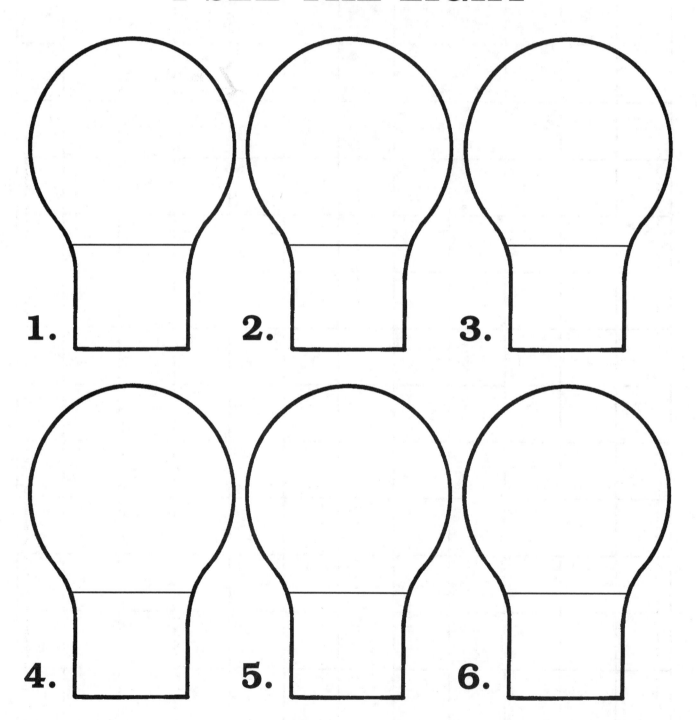

To the teacher: *Duplicate one copy of the page and write your questions in one part of each bulb before duplicating a set for the children. They will write their response to your question in the other part.*

Name _____ Date_____

Book Title _____

MAKE A MATCH

To the teacher: *Duplicate one copy of the page and write your question in the left box before duplicating a set for the children. They will write their response to your question in the box on the right.*

PENCIL IT IN

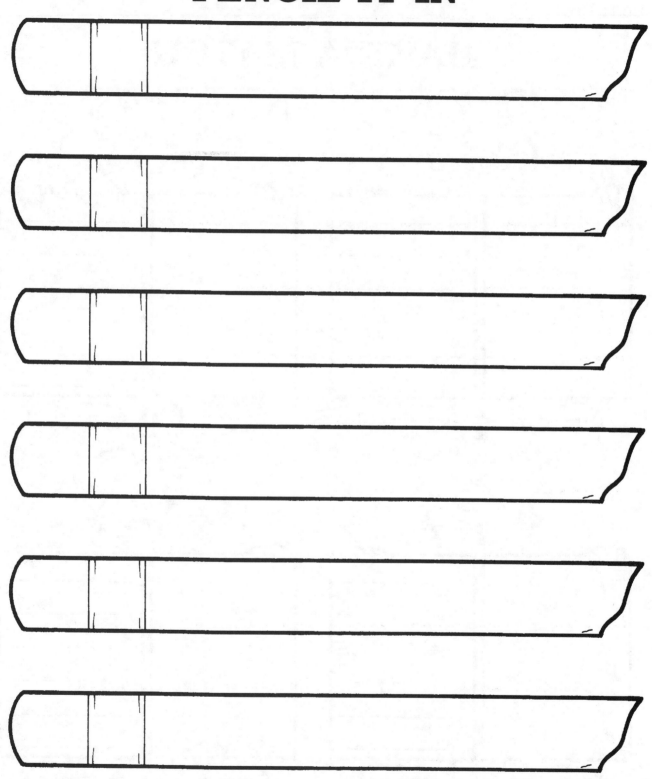

To the teacher: *This and the following page are a pair. Duplicate one copy of each page and write your question on half the pencil and the answer on another half. Then, duplicate a set for the children. They will cut, match, and paste. OR write only your question and have the children print the answer before cutting and pasting.*

PENCIL IT IN (cont.)

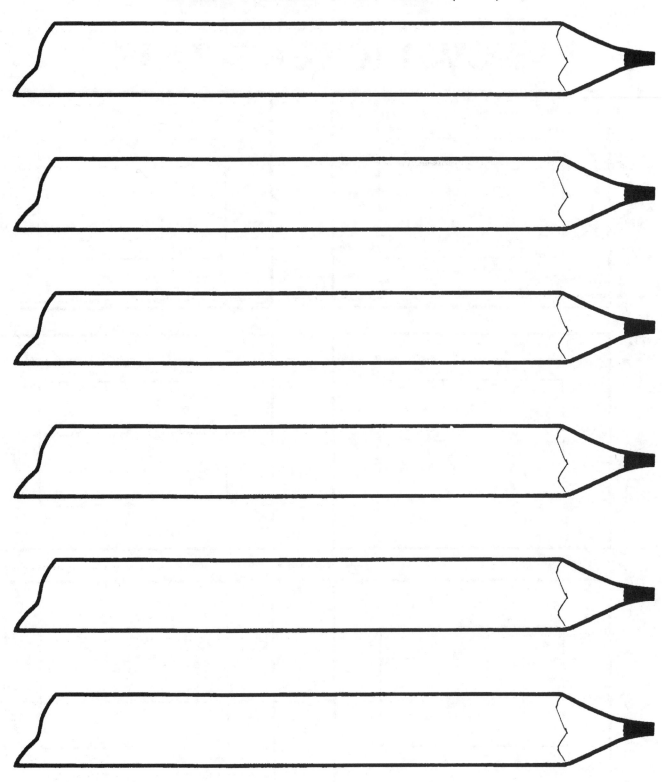

Teacher Resource

Name _____ Date _____

Book Title _____

NOW PICTURE THIS

1.

2.

3.

4.

5.

6.

To the teacher: *Duplicate one copy of the page and write your question in the frame before duplicating a set for the children. They will draw their response to your question in the center of each frame.*

#147 Activities for Any Literature Unit

122

©*1995 Teacher Created Materials, Inc.*

BOOK PROJECTS

Your students will enjoy doing a variety of book projects to enhance their enjoyment of literature. These may be independent, group, or class activities.

FROM READING TO WRITING

A familiar story can lead into creative writing activities.

- If the book is wordless, write a version with words.

- If there is a text, create a picture version to be shared with a younger brother or sister.

- Create a class book of opinions about a given story.

- Use information in the book to develop a counting or ABC book.

- Write an innovation, changing characters, setting, and/or events.

- Write a sequel. What happens next?

- Rewrite the story including a part for the reader.

- Rewrite the story with a new ending.

- Read the story to a certain point, and then allow the children to predict and write the ending.

CHOOSING A FORMAT

There are several types of books from which to choose. By providing your students with a variety of options, you will help keep their book-publishing projects fresh and interesting.

On the following pages are ideas for different forms of individual or class publications. Certain titles lend themselves to a specific book project. Therefore, think about the adaptability before you make a choice. In some situations, you will have to take a large part in constructing the book or guiding the children through the directions.

BOOK PROJECTS *(cont.)*

WHEEL BOOK

Materials: circle pattern, construction paper or tagboard, crayons, scissors, brad

Directions:

1. Make two copies of the circle pattern. Cut out both.

2. Cut the slice out of *one* wheel only.

3. Attach the two circles at their centers with a brad.

4. Have the children draw a picture or write about something from their story in the window.

5. Direct them to turn the wheel and write or draw in each space.

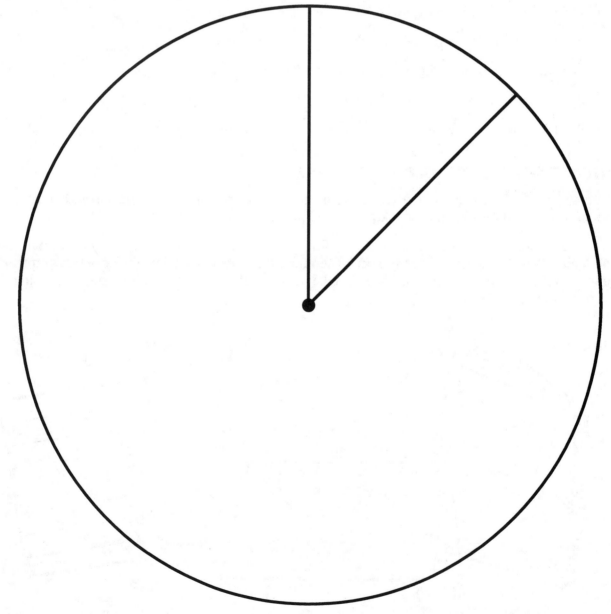

124

BOOK PROJECTS *(cont.)*

BIG BOOK

These are simple to make and particularly good for group or class projects.

Materials: construction paper 18" x 24" (45cm x 60cm), lined writing paper cut in strips no more than 18" (45 cm) in length, white unlined paper 8½"x11" (22 cm x 28 cm), scissors, glue, hole punch, metal rings, crayons, colored pencils, or markers

Directions:

1. Each child in the group is given a strip of lined paper on which you have written an event from the story. More capable learners may write their own sentences.

2. The children are instructed to glue their strips to the bottom of sheets of construction paper.

3. Each illustrates his event on the white unlined paper.

4. The illustration is glued to the top of the construction paper.

5. The children arrange the pages in order.

6. The group designs a cover.

7. Punch holes on the left side of each page and bind the big book together with metal rings.

8. Put the big books in your class or school library.

SHAPE BOOK

Book covers and writing pages can be made in any shape appropriate to the theme of the story.

Materials: tagboard, writing paper, stapler, scissors, crayons

Directions:

(If you have access to a cutter with various templates you will not need all of the following directions.)

1. Trace your pattern on tagboard and cut it out.

2. Use this as a pattern to cut the pages in the same shape.

3. Cut as many pages as desired.

4. Make covers of construction paper. Have the children decorate them.

5. When the children have written or drawn on the pages, staple the pages in order between the covers.

BOOK PROJECTS *(cont.)*

ORIGAMI MINI-BOOK

Materials: sheet of paper or light construction paper, scissors

Directions:

1. Fold the paper into eight boxes and open it again.

2. Holding the paper vertically, refold it down over the first fold and cut the paper as shown only to the next fold.

3. Open the paper and turn it horizontally. Fold it down and begin pushing both ends toward the middle.

4. You will notice that the center begins to pop out. Keep pushing until you have pushed it flat.

5. Turn all sides the same direction, and you have an instant book.

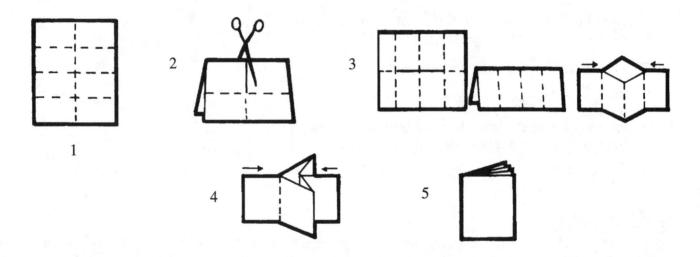

ACCORDION BOOK

This style of book is useful for counting or ABC books.

Materials: a long strip of butcher or shelf paper, scissors, tagboard, tape

Directions:

1. Fold a sheet of butcher paper in half lengthwise.

2. Accordion fold the paper into several equal sections.

3. Insert a piece of tag board into each end to help support the book and tape the edges so it is secure inside.

4. Draw lines on the folds.

5. Assign groups of children to draw or write on the panels.

6. Refold the book to store.

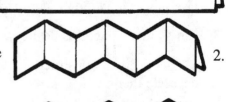

BOOK PROJECTS *(cont.)*

POP-UP BOOK

Materials: construction paper or unlined writing paper, scissors, crayons

Directions:

1. Fold the paper in half crosswise.

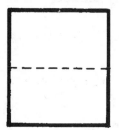

2. Cut two slits no more than half-way down from the fold.

3. Push the cut area through the fold and crease it to reveal the pop-up.

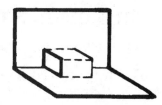

4. Have children draw, color, and cut out something from the story to glue to the pop-up.

5. They may complete the background and add a text to the page if directed.

6. When several pages are completed, they may be glued together. (One child can make several pages for his own book, or it can be a group project.) Make sure the pop-up sections are free.

7. Glue a cover to the book and decorate.

STEP BOOK

These books are particularly useful for organizing sequential information or writing directions.

Materials: four sheets of paper, stapler

Directions:

1. Place four sheets of paper on top of one another, overlapping the ends.

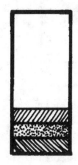

2. Hold the pages together and fold them forward so that eight steps are formed.

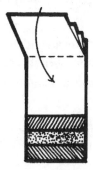

3. Crease and staple across the top.

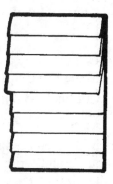

BOOK PROJECTS *(cont.)*

FLIP-UP BOOK (page 129)

Directions:

1. On the top three panels have the children draw three pictures in sequence from the story.
2. Then, they write about each picture on the lines below.
3. Finally, they flip panels open one at a time to read the story to a friend.

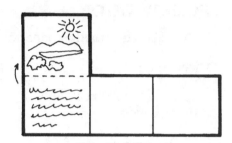

FOLD-OVER-AND-OVER BOOK (pages 130 and 131)

This is a book the children enjoy manipulating.

Materials: two copies of page 130 and one copy of page 131 for each child, (If possible, use three colors of paper.) invisible tape, scissors

To prepare:

1. Cut out the three pages and cut into the center where indicated.
2. Stack the three pages with the lines facing down. Note the *last* page has lines on only half the square. These should be on your left-hand side.
3. Fold the pages into quarters and then unfold again.

To assemble: At first the directions may seem complicated, but once you catch on it is quite simple! You are going to fold in a clockwise direction.

1. Fold down the *top right quarter* of the first page. Label it "1."

2. Use invisible tape to tape the top left quarter of the first page to the top right quarter of the second page which is now visible.

3. Now fold the *bottom right quarter* of the first page (now doubled) to the left. Label it "2."

4. Fold the bottom left quarter of the page up. Label it "3."

5. Fold the top left quarter across to the right. Label it "4."

6. Now fold down the top right quarter of the second page. Label it "5."

7. Use invisible tape to tape the top left quarter of the second page to the top right quarter of the third page, which is now visible.

8. Continue folding the pages in a clockwise direction, labeling as you go until you reach "10."

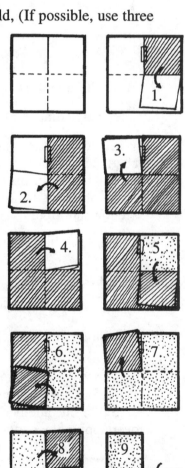

The children can reopen their books. Use the top page for title and illustration and write their story on pages 1–10.

BOOK PROJECTS *(cont.)*

FLIP-UP BOOK

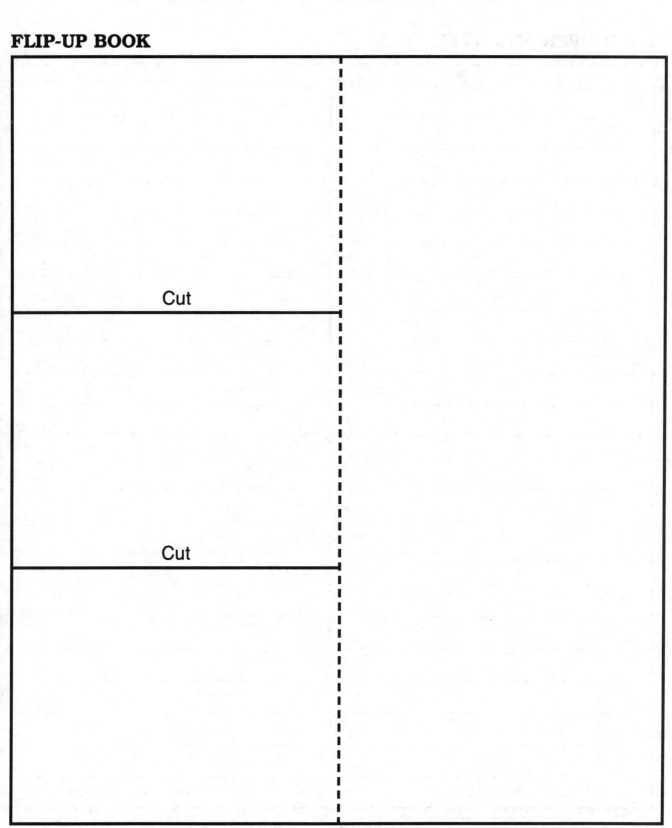

Cut

Cut

Fold Down

BOOK PROJECTS *(cont.)*

FOLD-OVER-AND-OVER BOOK

cut →

To the teacher: *Duplicate two copies for each book you are making.*

BOOK PROJECTS *(cont.)*

FOLD-OVER-AND-OVER BOOK *(cont.)*

cut→

To the teacher: *Duplicate one copy for each book you are making.*

BOOK PROJECTS *(cont.)*

These next two pages show you some easy ways to bind books.

Simple Binding

Materials: large construction paper or other heavy paper, scissors, white masking tape or book-binding tape, stapler, yarn and 3-hole punch and hole reinforcers (optional)

Directions:

1. Put the story pages in order.
2. Fold the construction paper in half to make a cover.
3. Place the story pages between the covers and staple along the left side (1).
4. Fold the tape over both sides of the staples to cover them (2).

1.   2.

Option: Instead of stapling the paper edges together, punch holes on the left side of each page. Attach hole reinforcers to the front and back of each hole. Thread yarn through the holes and tie.

Taped Binding

Materials: story pages, scissors, electrical or duct tape

Directions:

1. Start with the last page of the story and work from back to front.
2. Place the last page on a flat surface.
3. Use book-binding tape to tape the left side of the page to the flat surface (1).
4. Place the next-to-last story page on top of the previous page.
5. Use the book binding tape to tape down the left side of the page (2).
6. Continue in this same manner until all pages and the cover have been taped.
7. Lift up all the pages and fold the tape edges around the back pages (3).
8. Cover the binding with a wide tape such as electrical or duct tape (4).

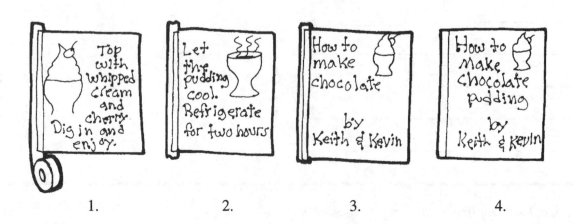

1.   2.   3.   4.

BOOK PROJECTS *(cont.)*

Book Covers

This type of cover offers a more permanent and durable way to cover books.

Materials: cardboard or tag board, scissors or utility knife, cloth, canvas, wallpaper or other durable fabric, scissors, glue, needle and thread or dental floss, paper

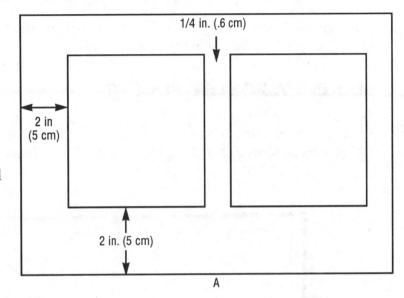

A

Directions

1. Cut two pieces of cardboard or tag board ½ inch (1.25 cm) larger than than the pages of the book to be bound. These two pieces will be the covers.

2. Lay the cover material (cloth, canvas, wallpaper, etc.) with its pattern facing down on a flat surface.

3. Place the covers ¼ inch (.6 cm) apart on the cover material. Cut the cover material so there is a 2 inch (5 cm) border around the covers (A).

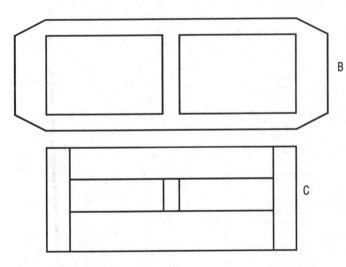

B

C

4. Clip a triangular piece from each corner of the cover material (B).

5. Fold the edges of the material over the covers and glue (C).

6. Fold over and glue the top and bottom edges in the same manner.

7. Collate the pages of the book to be bound.

8. With needle and thread (or dental floss) stitch no more than six pages at a time down the center of the cover.

9. After all pages have been sewn to the cover, glue the first page to the left inside cardboard cover. Glue the last page to the right inside cardboard cover (D).

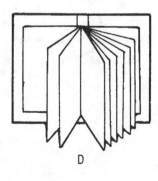

D

POETRY APPRECIATION

Children love poetry. They enjoy listening to a poem read over and over, reciting one along with you or to another person, and reading one on their own.

MAKING A POETRY POCKET

One way of developing an appreciation of poetry is to present each child with his own "poetry pocket." Duplicate the patterns on this and the following page. You and/or your children can cut out the patterns and glue as directed. They should be laminated for a longer lifespan!

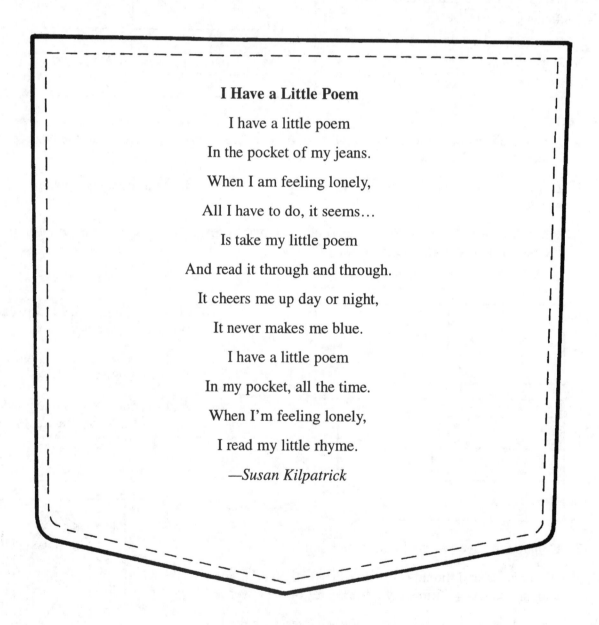

I Have a Little Poem

I have a little poem

In the pocket of my jeans.

When I am feeling lonely,

All I have to do, it seems…

Is take my little poem

And read it through and through.

It cheers me up day or night,

It never makes me blue.

I have a little poem

In my pocket, all the time.

When I'm feeling lonely,

I read my little rhyme.

—*Susan Kilpatrick*

Glue this piece on top.

POETRY APPRECIATION *(cont.)*

MAKING A POETRY POCKET *(cont.)*

Here are some ideas for filling the Poetry Pocket.

1. Make copies of several poems and staple them together. Encourage the children to read them aloud. As they learn each poem, they add it to their poetry pockets.

2. Duplicate short poems on colored paper. (They can be laminated if you desire.) Distribute one a week and encourage the children to read it over and over.

3. Display several poetry books at a center or library area. Encourage the children to copy a favorite poem each week and add it to their pockets.

Do not glue along this side.

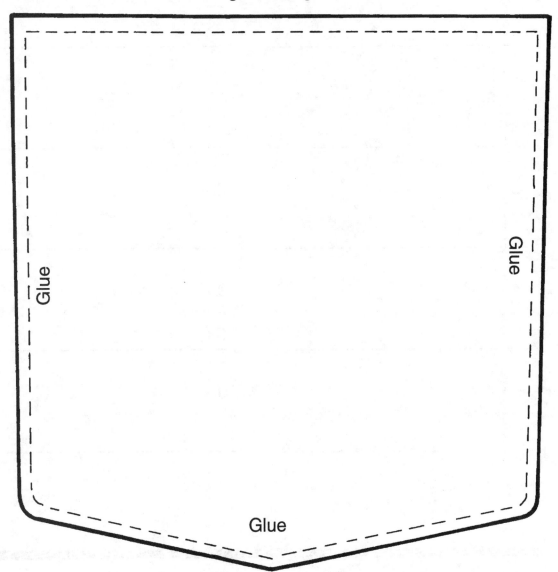

This piece forms the back of the pocket.

POETRY APPRECIATION *(cont.)*

POETRY BREAK

These are the poems I listened to or read aloud.

1. _____

2. _____

3. _____

4. _____

5. _____

6. _____

7. _____

8. _____

9. _____

10. _____

To the teacher: *The students may read to someone at home or perhaps a classmate during a short break.*

POETRY APPRECIATION (cont.)

FAVORITE POETRY BOOKS

Joanna Cole

A New Treasury of Children's Poetry

Lee Hopkins

Pterodactyls and Pizza

Eve Merriam

It Doesn't Always Have to Rhyme

Jamboree: Rhymes for All Times

A Sky Full of Poems

Blackberry Ink

Jeff Moss

The Other Side of the Door

Mary O'Neill

Hailstones and Halibut Bones

Jack Prelutsky

Something Big Has Been Here

The New Kid on the Block

Ride a Purple Pelican

Zoo Doings—Animal Poems

It's Halloween

It's Thanksgiving

It's Christmas

It's Valentine's Day

Maurice Sendak

Chicken Soup With Rice

Shel Silverstein

Where the Sidewalk Ends

A Light in the Attic

Collections

The Random House Book of Poetry

Sing a Song of Popcorn

TO HELP YOU DRAW

TO HELP YOU DRAW (cont.)

TO HELP YOU DRAW (cont.)

TO HELP YOU DRAW (cont.)

TO HELP YOU DRAW (cont.)

This
Super Reader Award
is presented to

_____

for

reading _____ books.

Congratulations!

_____
Teacher

_____
Date

Name _____ Date _____

I ♥ TO READ!

These are the best books I have read this year!

Title _____

Author _____

Title _____

Author _____

Title _____

Author _____

Title _____

Author _____

Title _____

Author _____